MYSTICS IN THE MAKING

MYSTICS IN THE MAKING

LAY WOMEN IN TODAY'S CHURCH

Carolyn Humphreys, O.C.D.S., O.T.R.

GRACEWING

First published in England in 2012
by
Gracewing
2 Southern Avenue
Leominster
Herefordshire HR6 0QF
United Kingdom
www.gracewing.co.uk

ISBN 978 085244 780 2

Typeset by Gracewing

To Mary of Nazareth, who shows us the way

TABLE OF CONTENTS

ACKNOWLEDGEMENTS

My heartfelt appreciation and sincere gratitude are graciously extended to the following women: Nancy Shuman, Jennifer Chang, Peg McKnight, Debi Hoppe, Carrie Warren, Iris Ruiz, Mary Bombace, Janet Tanner and Ida Rubin. Their useful comments, helpful suggestions and experiential wisdom were essential in bringing this book to reality.

The following poems in *Mystics in the Making* came from a small book edited by Kenneth Christopher, *A Sampler of Devotional Poems* (Mahwah, NJ: Paulist Press).

Bernard of Clairvaux, 'Jesus thou Joy of Loving Hearts', used in chapter 3.

Francis X Connolly, 'I Thank Thee Lord for This Good Life', used in chapter 4.

Teresa of Avila, 'Oh When a Soul is Hid in Thee', used in chapter 7.

Robert Hugh Benson, 'What Hast Thou Learnt Today', used in chapter 9.

Chapter Eight, 'When the Cupboard is Bare' contains the article 'On Loss' by Carolyn Humphreys, which was printed in *Spirituality*, Volume 9, Number 48 (May/June 2003), published by the Dominican Friars, Dominican Publications, Dublin, Ireland. Used with permission of the Editor, Father Tom Jordan, OP.

FOREWORD

Mystics in the Making: Lay Women in Today's Church is a spiritual feast for contemporary lay women seeking to experience mystical intimacy with God. Throughout the pages of this book, the threads of ordinary living, ordinary moments, and ordinary people are woven through a tapestry of the supernatural opportunity presented by Christ for us to live a transcendent life — to become 'Mystics in the Making'. Accordingly we observe that what is apparently ordinary serves an extraordinary purpose when illuminated by God's light and love. And that is just the beginning of the 'Good News' proclaimed in this joyous book, another by Carolyn Humphreys, O.C.D.S., author of *From Ash to Fire* and *Carmel, Land of the Soul*. Carolyn invites us to consider the spiritual heights to which God calls us, and the ladder gently lowered for our ascent to the summit. Carolyn draws us into a dialogue, which challenges us to revisit foundational beliefs and inferences, and to open ourselves to growth through divine transformation.

The timing is ideal for the publication of *Mystics in the Making*. In our stress-filled society, many women are living with one foot in yesterday, and one foot in tomorrow, and negating their potential for peace and happiness today.

Moreover, it is sad but true, that many seeking a deeper spiritual life are not aware of the vast potential, which lies within them, to find a deeper union with the Triune God through following 'simple' interior steps to holiness. Of course, we want to take these steps because, as Carolyn reminds us, 'Each of us is unique and we can only find our authentic identity in God. Jesus tells us who we really are; and to this we must listen.'

But, ah, there lies a paradox within mystics in the making! Because of our human nature, those seemingly 'simple' steps to holiness often tax us and demand greater humility and selflessness than we can muster alone. To better understand our shortcomings and character flaws, Carolyn compassionately takes us back to the beginning of the development of our personalities, our egos, and our mindsets, and traces the relationship between attitude and action. In doing so, it becomes clear to us why we frequently fail to assume our mystic identity, in spite of our best intentions. Due to these poor attitudes, we lack the necessary levels of love and trust, the 'guideposts' for mystics.

But all is certainly not lost. Throughout *Mystics in the Making*, we are reminded of how very much we are loved by God. We have been given many guides to enable us to live in mystical friendship with Jesus Christ. Chief among these guides are: holy scripture, the Church, our blessed mother, the Carmelite saints, grace, contemplative prayer, spiritual friendships and community. Add to these guides the sacraments that cement our friendship with Jesus, especially the holy Eucharist and reconciliation. And we must not forget the useful tools and virtues that are especially made manifest in an atmosphere of prayer and self knowledge. They include: faith, love, hope, mystery, perseverance, self-respect, humility, suffering, work, sacrifice, silence, solitude, wonder and laughter.

The extent to which all of these gifts are experienced and utilized to affect our behavior in a manner commensurate with the will of God is directly related to the intensity of our prayer lives. As we deepen our prayer lives, so shall we expect to see the way we live transformed. Carolyn tells us 'The warmth of our prayer and the light from our good works makes God easier to find in our society.' Thus, the 'icing on the cake' for mystics is creating a better world through interior transformation.

Ida Marie Rubin, O.C.D.S.

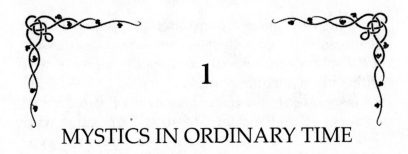

1

MYSTICS IN ORDINARY TIME

Once upon a time a little girl was walking home with her beloved father. It was night and as she gazed up at the stars, peacefully twinkling in the sky, she was struck with wonder. A cluster of stars that resembled pearls, gave her great joy because they were formed in a 'T', the first letter of her name—Therese. She pointed them out to her papa and exclaimed 'Look, Papa, my name is written in heaven.' What a blessed sign of God's tender love. Therese's interpretation of her stars showed her communion and fascination with the Triune God. Her childlike trust in God and innocent wonder at his creation were beautiful to behold. These two traits were manifest as she continued to look up at her 'T' while she walked on the sidewalk, and remained prominent throughout her life.

In time this little girl became known as Therese of Lisieux, the most beloved saint of modern times. She continues to teach her little way to God to millions of people. She shows us how to live a transcendent life, connecting God and his creation, earth and heaven. She helps us to see how our names are written in the heart of God and how we should have complete confidence in him. She urges us on: 'We must not be discouraged by our faults for children fall frequently... The memory of my faults humbles me; it causes me never to rely on my own strength, which is but weakness, but especially it teaches me a further lesson of the mercy and love of God.' Her confidence was neither blind nor automatic, but trusting and absolute. She responded to the call of Jesus wholeheartedly and invites us to do the same. Her total cooperation with God's graces was life long; a loving legacy for us to emulate. 'Wherever is a little one let him come to me' were words of Jesus very dear to her. God was her strength and her song. She, the exemplary little one, sang the mercies of the Lord with her whole life. She teaches us about the ocean of God's mercies, and how we should float on this ocean in our little boat named 'Gratitude'.

So all who are Christian mystics must sing of the mercies of the Lord. A mystic woman often shows the mercy of Jesus by her willingness and readiness to help others. She reaches out to others with a loving heart, compassionate eyes and warm hands. Courage, strength, gentleness and kindness are woven into the mystery that is known as woman. Womanhood, at its best, stands for all that is pure, noble, true, good and beautiful. A good woman's price is above rubies; she is worth more than all the riches of the world. The beauty of femininity is one of God's greatest gifts. Together with the mystical component woven within and around us, femininity is something very exquisite, and can never be fully understood.

Above all a mystic woman is a God seeker. She seeks God in such a way that her duties of life are not neglected, jeopardized or postponed. Rather, these duties are used as a means for her holiness. Her companion and guide in the pursuit of holiness is the person of Jesus Christ. In the midst of her busy life, she sets aside some time each day for quiet prayer with him. This time, usually in the early morning and/or late evening when the house is quiet and still, is a sacred time. This sacred time becomes more precious as her friendship with Jesus deepens. A fixed time for prayer is a blessed way to start and end the day. Other activities are energized and sanctified by prayer, which is the primary ingredient that makes the day holy. During morning meditation a mystic wife and mother entrusts her loved ones to God's care, protection and guidance during the day. In the evening she blesses her children with the sign of the cross on their foreheads when she tucks them in at bed time. She realizes how important daily prayers with her husband and children are. She also knows that nothing equals a mother's prayers for her children. Daily prayer is simple, without frills or sparkles, somewhat like Jesus' was when he went into the desert in the early morning and prayed to his Father.

Thoughts and words are few about our mystical make up. We share our consolations in prayer or experiences of God with a trusted few. We do not have all the answers, solutions or questions. We are notorious for starting over after we have made a mistake. We are not concerned about where we are on the mystical landscape, or if we are a mystic at all. Becoming a mystic is a gift from God, and who the real mystics are is known only by him.

In this book, feminine pronouns have been used for the sake of simplicity and ease of reading. Men who read this book are welcome to replace feminine pronouns with masculine ones as there is a mystical dimension within each one of us. Rooted in what is truly real, this dimension shows the first signs of life when the duties of religion become more than just something else that needs to be done. To a certain extent, and with the workings of grace, we have a responsibility to cultivate the interior soil of our soul so that it will nurture the growth of mystical seeds that God plants in us.

Essentials on the Spiritual Journey

The two most necessary virtues that are needed to keep us moving ahead on our journey to mystical union with God are humility and self knowledge. Teresa of Avila was adamant about this. Humility is the forerunner of all virtues. Through it, we see ourselves as we stand before God and before others. We grow in our appreciation of all life. Humility keeps us grounded in God by illuminating what is artificial in our lives and by shining the light of truth on perplexing situations. We strive in the best way we can toward what seems right. We keep to a sound middle course by walking with prudence. We do not act like no nothings or act out with excessive zeal. Humility quiets our hearts despite extreme difficulties or complexities in our home, workplace or personal circumstances. Our family life can resemble storm surf, dancing waves, placid seas or any oceanic movement in between. Humility is the rudder that guides our family lifeboat safely on its seafaring journey. Our spiritual life does not exist outside, below, above or alongside the other dimensions of our lives. Rather, it is the nucleus of our being, the source from which our other dimensions thrive. We find God within us as well as within the poorest of persons, no matter in what area his or her poverty expresses itself. Humility helps us accept who we are before God and reach out in a positive way to life's circumstances. These circumstances, as strange as they may be, contain elements for our spiritual growth.

Self knowledge can grow in us until we are under the sod and the dew pushing up daisies. The layers of ego are removed which is a painful and frightening process. When we think about the great mysteries of God, we learn about our own lowliness and continual need for God's mercy. Self knowledge helps us to accept our limitations without self pity, to work with them and perhaps through them. By trying our best, we learn how God can use anything to free us from the prisons of our egos. When we avoid being unrealistic about what we can accomplish, we watch for signs that show us we are over burdened, over extended, annoyed or tired. We stop before we are taxed beyond our strength. We take care of what we own and do not live beyond our means. The drawbacks of too much stuff help us to control our purchases. How often do we use what we bought? The futility of endless discussions and speculations helps us control our tongues. Most people like to talk and slips of the tongue can happen in an instant. Who hasn't made a few of these slips? How often do we reflect on the full implications of what we say? Frequently, it is not what we say, but how we say it that causes trouble. Our words can take a back seat to our gestures, voice tone and inflections. Through sound self discipline we control our speech and behavior, strengthen our self respect and channel our energies to activities that change things for the better.

Good self discipline influences each decision we make and how we act on that decision, as well as how we react to life's circumstances. Everyday decisions and circumstances deepen or diminish our relationship with God. They also foster or hinder love for ourselves and for others.

An important attribute for the mystic is the ability to listen. If we do not listen to others, how can we listen to God, who often speaks in whispers? When we listen to our family, those who are poor, ill or who live alone, we may be eager to help them. In our rush of helpful hints and plans that will 'fix things', and in our excitement about getting our message across by sharing what happened to us, we may just ruin things. We need do something else before we jump into our action mode. We need to extend a loving presence through listening. Listening is a prerequisite for action. If we immediately launch into an explanation of ways to meet a specific need, it could distance or perhaps patronize the person we wish to help. If we are inspired to be loquacious, we might reflect on this old English saying: 'A wise old owl sat in an oak. The more he heard, the less he spoke. The less he spoke, the more he heard. Why can't we all be like that bird?'

It takes more courage to be in the dark, with someone who is in the dark, than it does to stand outside the dark and talk about the light. What we think of as our bright lights of knowledge may be of no use if we speak about them while standing in the midday sun. Just to sit in the dark twilight of someone's suffering and to share their pain by listening with the heart creates a caring climate. We need to be with someone before doing for that someone because acting may not be the most important thing to do. On the contrary, action may even shelter us from the powerlessness we feel when we are helpless and can do nothing. A quiet time to be present, with nothing more than a hand to hold, or a shoulder on which to cry, seems so simple yet may mean so much to the person in need. A healing presence may bring forth in the other person his or her inner resources, evoking a desire to take the next good step, and stimulating a will to live which looks beyond present limitations.

Candle Flames of Hope

In today's world, true mysticism often goes unnoticed, or is presented in unsuitable or erroneous ways. This is regrettable, because mysticism is that element by which we experience life at its fullest breath, width, height and depth. There is an interesting paradox at this point. We cannot go to the deepest center of ourselves, where the Triune God dwells, unless we go entirely out of ourselves in selfless service to others. The degree of love shown in our service to others is the degree by which we are also a mystic. Stay at home moms (or stay at home dads) excel in the service of love by creating a good home where those in it are cared for, strengthened and encouraged, and where everyday duties are done in a responsible and Christ like manner. Grandparents, maiden aunts and single cousins often provide necessary fortification for parents who are raising children. Parent's sincere words of love and praise to their children are worth more than gold. This also holds true for teachers, and other adults who resemble parent figures. Service to our family is just as dear to the heart of God as the service of those who are away from the home front in special mission fields. When we realize this, there is rarely a need to call attention to ourselves or to what we do, or to be noticed by what we wear, what we say or how we act. All work is important to the heart of God. It is not what we do but how we do it. The intention which underlies our work, and how we work, comes from the quality of our prayer. Prayer increases our ability to love. Love is made visible in our work.

Although the word mystic can have peculiar connotations, a mystic who is a God seeker is really not a strange bird. He or she is commonplace, more like a plain brown sparrow pecking in the dirt in the heat of midday, than a red breasted robin singing sweetly in the coolness of dawn. Or, to put it in a kitchen setting, more like common table salt that sprinkles everything with God's love, than a rare spice that gives a specific flavor to a few foods. One is unobtrusive and has one's feet on the ground. There is no need to say wise and wonderful things at the perfect time. True mystics are not phonies, nor do they have 'show time' tendencies. They are authentic 'real deals' who have practical skills, common sense, home spun wisdom and a light hearted sense of humor. Far from being in a dream like, misty trance, they are aware, alert and informed. They are direct in speech and refrain from pious phrases and pat answers. Love and trust are their guideposts. Love grows from trust that accepts what cannot be changed, what is unknown in life, and what is hurting in the self and in the other.

We know there is no such thing as the perfect mystic. Each of us has unknown realms and hidden pain. We all have our sins, our faults, our moments, our good days and our bad days. The positive thing is that we don't all have our bad moments at the same time. We give respected space to those who are having difficulties. We pray for them, do what we can and then let God take his time to work in them. We are all weak and vulnerable. There are always little tensions, disagreements and altercations that cast small passing shadows on family interactions, but they are rarely a big deal. The difference lies within us. The mystic ponders what is going on around or within her in the light of God's goodness. She strives to be aware of his divine presence in everything. What is stagnant and ordinary to others emanates with God's mystery and wonder to her. She delights in the wonder of little things: eating a brownie, singing a silly song, hearing the birds chirp, watching the rainfall, patting a kitten or smelling a rose. In creative moments she might imagine people of all ages to be like flowers blossoming in a garden, each with its own unique color, hue, size, shape and scent. To know roses, (the wise women in her life) is to know the beauties of God. To know that the faded roses, (wise women who are very ill or who have died) will bloom again is to believe in the beauty of heaven. She is captivated by the many expressions of God's love around her. His love enables her to laugh with ease, roll with the punches of life and maintain a tender regard for those with troubles. During difficult times she may interiorly question: 'Where is Jesus in all of this?' Then she realizes how that which troubles or irritates her can bring her face to face with God. Indeed, even a brush with death can be a blessing in disguise. Sometimes we need a good shake to move us out of our comfort zones and look at life with a fresh perspective.

As mystical women, single or married, we are pilgrims of faith who participate in our call to holiness through our nobility and personal uniqueness. We bear witness to faith through prayer, love and service. We perceive life as a journey to God. We walk forward on this sacred path by making choices that respond to God's love for us. These choices are based on gospel values and the Magisterium of the Church. We become the people we are called to be by seeking God in all things and making it a life habit to live in imitation of Jesus Christ. When God takes over our lives, we learn to take one step at a time and know the journey will not end on this earth.

Rooted in Faith

The Holy Trinity is the central mystery of our faith. The Triune God dwells within us and directs our lives. God is the source of truth, beauty, goodness, wisdom and love. We ponder God's attributes and seek to infuse them into our living situation. We believe in God the Father, creator of all, who is almighty, eternal, incomprehensible and infinite. We believe in Jesus Christ, the only Son of God, who was born of the Virgin Mary by the power of the Holy Sprit. Jesus shows us the way to God the Father. He is the Messiah, our Lord and Savior, the Redeemer of all humankind. We believe in the Holy Spirit who proceeds from the Father and the Son and who assists us with discernment. The Holy Spirit sanctifies us and strengthens us so that we become authentic followers of Jesus. Mary, the strongest and most feminine of all women, is our model and guide in our lifelong journey to God. She helps us to find holiness in the ordinary activities of our days. Like her, we live in the mystery of faith. Mary shows us how to say yes to God no matter what happens. Mary's example keeps us moving forward with a holiness that does not allow for any illusions and is not for the faint of heart. Mary teaches us how to love by serving in little ways that go unnoticed at home, work and in other situations.

We grow in our union with God through reception of the sacraments, which are signs given to us by Jesus to help his life and love grow in us. We receive the sacrament of reconciliation regularly which shows us God's pardon, mercy and love and our need for repentance, reparation and conversion. Holy Communion is our closest encounter with the risen Lord. We receive the body, blood, soul and divinity of Jesus in this most blessed of sacraments. The Mass is our greatest prayer. We are blessed by the bread of life: the body of Christ. Jesus humbled himself to the point of disappearing under the appearance of bread. Transubstantiation is the total change of the substance of bread and wine into the substance of Christ's body and blood. Jesus is with us in the holy Eucharist. On Holy Thursday, Jesus graced a meal and elevated it to its highest honor. The Eucharist is the greatest sacrifice and most sacred meal of God's family. Holy Communion is the food we need most. Union with Christ in the Eucharist gives us indescribable peace in times of fragmentation and unrest.

The mystic in us experiences a reverence for all life. We seek to find the light of Christ in everyone. Each person is treated with dignity and respect. The gift of life is precious, from the moment of conception to natural death. Each life is sacred because it is made in the image and likeness of the living and holy God. A mother's long, prayerful watch at the bedside of her sick child tells us that life as we know it is good, difficult, fragile, sweet and transient. Therese of Lisieux says: 'The sufferings of Jesus pierced the heart

of his mother, so the sufferings and humiliations of the
ones we love the best on earth pierce ours.'

Each day we strive to know and love Jesus, who is
our solace and our shield, our rock secure on which
we build. He is our companion and our goal, our way,
truth and life. Mystics take to heart the words of John
Paul II:

> When you wonder about the mystery of your-
> self, look to Christ who gives you the meaning
> of life. When you wonder what it means to be
> a mature person, look to Christ, who is the
> fullness of humanity. Because actions speak
> louder than words, you are called to proclaim
> by the conduct of your daily lives that you
> really do believe that Jesus is the Lord.[1]

The Mountain and the Marketplace

Threads of Carmel's wisdom are woven through these
pages. The very essence of the Carmelite ideal is the
spirit and mystery of prayer, especially contemplative
prayer. The friars, nuns and secular members of this
order are pilgrims of prayer, ever moving on the slopes
of Mount Carmel. Mount Carmel is a symbol for the
spiritual adventure. This adventure is marked by roots
in the teachings of Jesus, growth in his love, and lived
out through all daily activities. The goal of all contemplative strivings is Christ the Lord. On their mountain
journey Carmelites gather the flowers and fruit of love
and contemplative prayer. They bring these flowers
and fruit down the mountain and give them away in
the marketplace. Quietly praying a Hail Mary for the
people in a long check out line, or saying a few words
of praise to a stressed out employee, are only a few of
many unobtrusive acts of holiness. These acts are small

signs of Christ's compassion within the ubiquitous business establishments of daily life. Striving for holiness has yet to be fully appreciated. It is not dull or boring. Nor is it an escape, withdrawal, denial or an ethereal state. Rather, it is an adventure that calls forth our most authentic self to live in love which definition goes beyond time, space and concept. John of the Cross takes us to the heart of holiness: 'The Father spoke one Word which was his Son, and the Word he speaks, ever in eternal silence and in silence must it be heard by the soul.'

The pursuit of holiness separates us from cultural and personal attitudes that support religious superstitions or blur what our Church teaches. Our values, principles and daily choices must change if they distance us from God's love. The Catholic contemplative/mystic way is not an assurance for health, wealth, psychological comfort or social or spiritual esteem. Nor does it shield us from the dark side of life or keep us in a naivete that is spiritually immature. It is not a security blanket that hides us from life's difficulties. It is much better than all of that. It sanctifies our relationships, work, play, and other components to create a balanced day.

Since the mystic journey is beyond ourselves, unity within our self is vital. All dimensions of our existence are motivated in one way or another during the mystic adventure. The quest for contemplative holiness kicks us out of our comfort zone. We pay attention to our loving Lord who moves gently within us and in those around us, though they may know it not. Teresa of Avila helps us along by telling us we must be daring in love, willing to take risks, and unafraid of looking foolish. Good family interaction involves both love and risk. Love is not authentic without risk.

An illness, problem, or negative situation is not something to use in order to get love, or to hide behind in order to live a 'risk less' life. Love helps parents talk about problems, but they watch what they say. Opposing views are expressed without doing harm. Parents know that habitual arguing in front of their children is not good. It may show that spousal love is at a low ebb or other problems. The children suffer from the fighting. (They also suffer when habitually spoken to in loud angry voices by adults.) Parents are their children's most powerful role models. They must not be afraid to reach out in faith to God, and to professionals, when they need help. This takes courage. Love is a decision that requires the most courage. Sometimes parents feel they only have a drop of courage. When this happens, they find peace in the courage of Christ. United with him, and relying on prompts from the Holy Spirit, parents have more strength than what can be imagined. The Christian family is so dependent on God. Cooperation with his grace carries them through hard times, frustrations and fears.

Teresa of Avila said that the Lord dwells among the pots and pans. In the kitchen, work resembles the hard, often unappreciated work of daily life. When the stress and tedium of routine chores wear us down, and composure begins to slip, we try to recall Teresa's words. As mystic women, we have no illusions of being better than others or part of a spiritually privileged coterie. We also try to avoid being the victim, the weeping willow, the shrinking violet, the drama queen, the anemic soul or the sad or sorry saint. Teresa was fond of asking God to save us from sour faced saints. A more refined authenticity comes from the hard work, prayer and grace that deepens our trust in God and moves us forward on the road to holiness. With hearts full of Teresa's 'determined determination' we possess an inner strength that makes it possible to stand up for our principles of holiness no matter what may happen to us.

Woman of Light

Edith Stein was born in Breslau on October 12, 1891, the youngest of eleven children. Her father died suddenly before she reached the age of two. Her mother raised the children and took over and managed her husband's lumber business. Edith was born into a Jewish family. She was a youthful atheist, mature philosopher, writer and teacher, convert to the Catholic faith, and, in her forty-second year she entered Carmel and became a nun. Along with her sister Rosa, she died at Auschwitz in 1942. The themes that seems to be most apparent throughout Edith's life are her integrity, her search for truth and her complete trust in God.

Edith was a brilliant scholar and quite ahead of her time regarding the role of women in society at that time. In a speech she delivered in Salzburg in 1930, she gave a masterful presentation on the differences between the natures of the male and the female. This may show why women are predisposed to walk on the mystical landscape. Women show more interest in persons than in objects. We can support this by watching men and women when they walk through a door and find only two things in a room: A cradle with a new born baby and a table with a new computer. Who goes to what? Most women would head for the baby and most men would head for the computer. Women seemingly place the concrete over the abstract and specifics over generalities. We admire the abstract in our lives; however, a person is more real than an idea. It is known that women respond more to relationships with people than to inanimate objects. Perhaps it is due to the 'mother bear wisdom' women intuitively possess. Christ is the life in our souls and women pass life on through nurturing and protecting others. Edith said that women are more interested in wholes than in parts. Women are less prone to dissect an animal or take apart a computer. They look at the whole forest more than the individual trees.

Now, men should not be dismayed or downhearted because the traits noted by Edith appear to be more common in women than in men. They can be common in men as well. We all know men who possess these traits and women who do not. There are virile men who work in kitchens, who excel in compassion and who are skilled in the caring arts. Mysticism is neither gender specific nor gender favored. It is an equal opportunity all inclusive dimension of life Edith's life was a quest for truth and for God. She helps us on our quest with these words:

> Who are you, sweet light, that fills me and illumines the darkness of my heart? You lead me like a mother's hand, and should you let go of me, I would not know how to take another step... Are you not the sweet manna that from the Son's heart overflows into my heart, the food of the angels and the blessed.[2]

The family is the heart of society. Home is the most beloved, and the most enduring, of all earthly establishments. The mystic shows by her life that, within her home, all things interconnect with God's graces and with each family member. These vital connections give greater strength, appreciation and reverence to the lifelong bonds that exist within the family unit. These bonds are rooted in God and are expressed by the family's love and concern for each other. The bonds reflect a transcendent goodness, confirmed by this prayer:

God made us a family.
We need one another.
We love one another.
We forgive one another.
We work together.
We worship together.
Together we use God's Word.
Together we grow in Christ.
Together we love all people.
Together we serve our God.
Together we hope for heaven.
These are our hopes and ideals.
Help us to attain them, O God,
Through Jesus Christ, our Lord. Amen.

Notes

1   Pope John Paul II, *Address to High School Students*, Madison Square Garden, New York (3 October 1979).

2   From St Teresa Benedicta of the Cross (Edith Stein), *Litany of the Holy Spirit*.

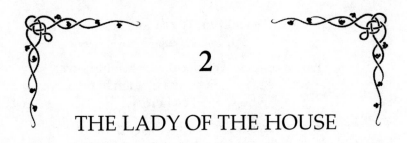

2

THE LADY OF THE HOUSE

'The Blessed Virgin, by becoming the Mother of God, received a kind of infinite dignity because God is infinite. This dignity, therefore, is such a reality that a better one is not possible, just as nothing can be better than God.'[1] These thought-provoking words were written by Thomas Aquinas. This lady of infinite dignity of whom he wrote, has made her loving presence known throughout Christian history.

In the thirteenth century a small band of lay hermits settled on Mount Carmel in Israel. They were former pilgrims, merchants, penitents and soldiers who wanted to live a simple, quiet life centered on the gospels and consecrated to Christ. They built a chapel to honor his mother, Mary, and took her for their patroness. They became known as the Brothers of the Blessed Virgin Mary of Mount Carmel. Around 1209 a rule was written for them by their bishop Albert, Patriarch of Jerusalem, which put together the elements of the life they were living. Thus the Carmelites became the first order dedicated to Mary in the Catholic Church. An ancient hymn, still sung today, tells of her love:

Flower of Carmel Tall vine blossom laden;
Splendor of heaven, Child bearing yet maiden,
None equals thee.
Mother so tender, Who no man didst know,

On Carmel's children Thy favors bestow.
Star of the Sea.

Strong stem of Jesse, Who bore one bright flower,
Be ever near us And guard us each hour,
who serve thee here.

Purest of lilies, That flowers among thorns,
Bring help to the true heart That in weakness turns
and trusts in thee.

Strongest of armor, We trust in thy might:
Under thy mantle, Hard pressed in the fight,
we call to thee.

Our way uncertain, Surrounded by foes,
Unfailing counsel You give to those
who turn to thee.

O gentle mother Who in Carmel reigns,
Share with your servants That gladness
you gained and now enjoy.

Hail, Gate of Heaven With glory now crowned,
Bring us to safety Where thy Son is found,
true joy to see.[2]

Mary is the heart of the Church. When Teresa of Avila fashioned a new form of life in Carmel, she placed a statue of Mary above the prioress's stall in the choir in order to remind her sisters who the real prioress of the house was. The choir is the place where the sisters gather several times a day for prayer. Teresa tells her nuns and us: 'Imitate Mary and consider how great she must be and what a good thing it is that we have her for our patroness.' We follow Teresa's example when Mary is at the heart of our homes. It is known that the heart has two movements: diastolic, the dilation of the cavities of the heart during which they fill with blood, and systolic, the contraction of the heart during which the blood is forced into circulation through the body. Mary always personifies these two movements. She receives grace from her Son, and pours it out on us. As long as we regard her as the Lady of our house, we will learn infinite things from her.

The first Carmelites called Mary 'the Lady of the place' because their chapel, which bore her name, was at the center of their scattered hermitages. Although 'lady of the house' is a familiar phrase, 'lady of the home' has an intimacy that is characteristic of Mary. Following the example of Teresa's placement of Mary's statue, it would be of great benefit if we had a statue of Mary in a prayer corner of our home. As the choir is a place for prayer in the cloister, so can our little shrine be a place of prayer, peace, and reflection in our home. The children in our home could be responsible for keeping the shrine tidy and decorating it with flowers on special days. Mary's corner would be a place of refuge for them as well as a place for family prayers such as the litany of Mary or the rosary. Because the rosary has a calming effect and a contemplative nature, it is a good prayer for busy family members. Mary's quiet corner would be a symbol of holiness in the home, which is often called the domestic church. It would remind us of Mary's faith, which shines like a beacon in a dark night. She lights the way for us, and beckons us to follow her. She takes us by the hand, helps us understand the true value of femininity in today's world, and assists us in being authentic women of God.

The longer we dwell on Mary's life, the more intriguing she becomes. We should remember the very primitive times in which she lived. What was her life like without electricity, running water, gas, lights, toilets, showers, a washing machine, sinks, a stove, TV, internet and cell phone? What was her kitchen like? How did she prepare meals? What were her favorite dishes? She worked hard, from the time she got up in the morning to the time she went to bed at night, with none of the modern conveniences we have today. If we researched Mary's way of life at Nazareth we would appreciate her much more, and would probably never complain about our housework again.

Mary moves our heart in unexpected ways and takes us deep into the mystery of God. She tenderly holds all mothers in her heart, not only mothers of children, but also women who care for the sick, poor, abandoned, neglected, uneducated and spiritually needy. Her silence teaches us many things about suffering, which is the lot of mothers. Her life is a long mystical journey. How well she shows us that mystics are deeply in love with God. She knew in her teens that she was the most favored one of the Lord. Did she know then, that there would be such a heavy price for this infinite dignity given to her by God? She made a promise: 'Let it happen to me as you say,' and she never strayed from her resolve. There were no compromises, there was no turning away. Ever.

A Gentle Heart

Mary teaches us the true meaning of meekness. To be meek is far from being a doormat, feeling useless or worthless, or having a poor self image. Self degrading or piteous comments about ourselves, or our concerns, are not marks of meekness. If we accept God as the creator of everything, including us, how can we see ourselves as worthless? Meekness has two defining elements: Sober self judgment in the light of gospel teachings and heart felt service according to our gifts and talents. Like Mary, we must not do less than what God wants of us. There is no weakness in meekness. Nor can we think so highly of ourselves that we end up being a disappointment to ourselves and others.

To learn to love in the school of Christ and not to be so hard on ourselves are the products of meekness. We see our weaknesses in the light of God. We work to overcome them, but do not get tangled up in them if they are not mastered. Our weaknesses, if not glaring, can be our road to salvation. God draws good from evil. We gain strength from weakness. God makes us complete in his own way and in his own time. Meekness is self effacing in the sense that we are not overly concerned with our interests, our goals and our points of view. Because we are emptied of pretense and exaggerated self respect we have the courage to risk failure. To try and to fail is better than to have never tried. We look around for things that need to be done and do them without fanfare. We are aware of how fragile we are and through that awareness can respond to the fragility of others. If a person is asked if she is doing her own will or the will of God, she will answer 'I do not really know. I hope I am doing God's will.' When an individual is doing God's will there is a sense of peace and well being. We ask Mary to help us accept whatever complexities tear our hearts or desolate our lives. We try to refrain from murmuring, sulking, rebelling, or resisting graces. God's will is manifested in our ability to make appropriate decisions based on the love of Christ. To do God's will is to let him love us, and let his love reach through us to other people.

On the streets Rose saw a small boy, cold and shivering in shabby, thin clothes. There was little hope of a decent meal for the child. Rose became angry and said to God, 'Why do you permit this? Why don't you do something about this?' That night God responded to Rose. Very softly she heard the words 'I certainly did do something about that. I made you.'

Many times Mary's eyes met with the eyes of her Son. During his passion their gaze held a bittersweet embrace. What wordless communication passed between them? How well mothers know this connection. What wordless communication passes between a mother and her child today? Soul stirring movements of the heart are not easily put into words. Mothers share this with Mary. She experienced the highest peaks and lowest depths of motherhood. She knew the greatest of joys, although the deepest of sorrows seemed to overshadow them. Several memories can tear apart a mother's heart. Mary's maternal hands tenderly caressed Jesus when he was a baby. They fed, clothed and cradled him. They covered him during cold nights. Her hands encouraged and supported him when he took his first steps and when she taught him how to pray. What were her heart's ponderings? What are the ponderings of mothers? Mary's routine tasks marked the simple and joyful passing of time at Nazareth: sweeping, washing, cooking, sewing. She could well have made Jesus a stuffed donkey with a whimsical smile and floppy ears. This donkey would be like the teddy bears of today that give quiet comfort, simple joy and many other good gifts to children young and old. A snuggly well worn teddy bear is worth more than words can say.

As mothers know, children can grow in grace and nature. The years pass by quickly and memories can be pleasant and comforting. Joseph's hands, strong and gentle, show Jesus how to craft wood. We can imagine how Mary enjoyed visiting them in Joseph's work area. A gentle scolding from Joseph when he saw Jesus playing with sharp tools, or a correction when he was teaching Jesus the art of carpentry, did not mar Mary's contentment when she visited them amid the sawdust and shavings. How the deep wound of separation must have pierced Mary's heart when Joseph died. Such a pain widows share with Mary upon the death of a beloved spouse. Bernard of Clairvaux points us in the right direction regarding Mary: 'In danger, in doubts, in difficulties, think of Mary, call upon Mary. Let her name depart from your lips; never allow it to leave your heart. And that you may more surely obtain the assistance of her prayer, don't neglect to walk in her footsteps.'

This is not an easy call. Mary's faith reached beyond her understanding all her life, and at the foot of the cross it seemed stretched beyond all limits. No one knows the depths of her lonely watch save God. She was the mother most tender, shrouded in unexplainable sorrow, who stood at the cross transfixed and transformed. Words from Jesus' dry parched lips gave her universal motherhood. At that moment, she moved from the embrace of one God child to the embrace of all humankind, from those she knew, to far flung strangers who do not know her son. She gathers all, then and now, into her sword pierced heart.

The ancient greyness shifted suddenly and thinned
Like mist upon the moors before a wind.
An old, old prophet lifted a shining face and said;

'He will be coming soon. The Son of God is dead;
He died this afternoon.'

A murmurous excitement stirred all souls.
They wondered if they dreamed —
Save one old man who seemed
Not even to have heard.

And Moses standing, hushed them all to ask
If any had a welcome song prepared.
If not, would David take the task?

And if they cared could not the three young children sing
The Benedicite, the canticle of praise
They made when God kept them from
perishing in the fiery blaze?

A breath of spring surprised them, stilling Moses' words.
No one could speak, remembering the first fresh flowers.
The little singing birds.

Still others thought of fields new ploughed
Or apple trees all blossom boughed.
Or some, the way a dried bed fills with water
Laughing down green hills.
The fisherfolk dreamed of the foam on bright blue seas.
The one old man who had not stirred remembered home.

And there He was splendid as the morning sun and
Fair as only God is fair.
And they, confused with joy, knelt to adore
Seeing that He wore five crimson stars
He never had before.

No canticle at all was sung.
None toned a psalm, or raised a greeting song.
A silent man alone of all that throng
Found tongue—not any other.

Close to His heart when the embrace was done,
Old Joseph said, 'How is your mother,
How is your mother, Son?'[3]

The Reed of God

Mary was a laywoman: a wife and a mother. Many women share Mary's suffering but no woman will equal her in the depths and breadth of her pain. She stood peerless in God's divine plan, a singularly privileged handmaid of the Lord. She never turned away from God. Mary's total openness and receptivity to the mystery of God's will was met with her ever present yes. Always. She offers to us the paradoxes of a life that is rooted and winged in love for her son: nothing and everything, emptiness and fullness, suffering and triumph, pain and glory. Mary always and forever points us toward her son. Jesus showed us the highest limits of love. He freely offered himself for us. The moment of his apparent failure was the moment of his ultimate glorification. Our loving amen to each shadow of the cross that overshadows our lives will be reflected in the joys of our alleluias in eternity. Mary is our best help to understand how the mystery of the cross is ever at the heart of our lives. The cross is a sign of ignominious suffering and the sign of brilliant triumph.

As women we are called to stand with Mary at the foot of the cross. This is a call that attracts and repels at the same time. Frenzied activities, comfort excesses, and ego padding insidiously draw us away from the side of Mary. We have no natural inclination to trod the blood marked footsteps of the Lord. Silently Mary motions for us to join her. She takes us beyond our own strength and infuses in us the desires of great love. She guides us through a barren and strange land that demands blind faith, stark simplicity and total vulnerability. With her, we are drawn into the obscurity of faith where things do not make sense, mystery is customary, and life is transformed. To walk through the mists on a trackless waste, void of pious sentiment, good feelings and devotional securities is frightening. Mary guides us with her wisdom. By her example we know that nothing on earth is ours forever. It seems we must lose that which we cannot keep in order to find what we cannot lose.

Mary's hands were always open to God. God cannot give what he wants to give us if our hands are full. Mary's hands were empty and look at what God put in them. God's love is something we cannot grasp or hold. It is something we treasure and give away. Mary shows us how to keep the difficult balance of rightfully valuing material things in our world and not allowing them to obscure God and his Providence. Does the trust we place in things we can see and hold outweigh the trust we have in God?

Hope is the secret source of our power to love. If carried with faith, our most overwhelming pain is bonded with immense hope. The passion of Jesus is like an ocean of love and mercy in which all our weakness and wickedness can disappear, like a drop in the ocean. When Jesus was on the cross, Mary gazed upon his face and saw the agonies of all her children. From the foot of the cross, Mary mirrored the forgiveness of her son. Her untold pain never turned to resentment or bitterness against those who were responsible for Jesus' death.

How often have we been hurt by a loved one who has done us wrong? Anger, pain and tension are so often in our homes. Life seems to be a continuous forgiveness of our family, friends, coworkers, enemies—and most of all, ourselves. We also need to forgive races, cultures, societies, governments and nations. Many times this is not easy. Mary shows us that forgiveness is based on love. The cross is the ultimate symbol of forgiveness. Without true forgiveness we cannot move forward. Forgiveness involves action. We must let go of that which causes us bondage. There is a soothing healing that comes after letting go. Forgiving others is an amazing grace. We forgive the hurt, and when it is remembered it is done so without recrimination, bitterness or revenge. Children can teach us much about forgiveness. They are naturals. They fight, and two minutes later they are friends again. Some grown ups hold on to grudges for dear life. They clutch slights and hurts as if they were treasures. They use pain in self-centered, negative ways and therefore are esteemed members of the 'Plum' Club (Poor Little Unfortunate Me). Mary teaches us to look and overlook, forget ourselves and give without strings, listen and be patient, forgive and be forgiven.

Every person is in need of forgiveness. She who cannot forgive destroys the path she must take in order to live the words of Jesus: 'Forgive us our trespasses as we forgive those who trespass against us.' If we are to grow spiritually, forgiving others is a constant. It frees us from the heavy burden of negative mind tapes that we replay over and over. Forgiveness of others is easier when we dwell on how often God forgives us. With courage we honestly face our recent choices in the light of God's love. Are our preferences more important to us than a good conscience? Our Church looks out for us, by trying to keep us out of trouble. Even when we do not agree with her teachings, we know that in the long haul of life, the Church is wise. How do we live what she teaches? How would we rate ourselves in our faithfulness to daily prayer, in keeping our word, in carrying out our responsibilities? How often do we make superficial excuses, indulge in idle chatter, or in diversions that are time wasters? When do we shout at our loved ones, or use abusive or condescending language? How do we accept inconveniences, maintain our boundaries and love others? When do we engage in hurtful or negative conversation, make snap judgments or tell derogatory jokes? When are we mediocre, domineering, deceptive, divisive or ungracious?

In the same vein we must look at and be thankful for our strong points: our talents, gifts, positive attributes, abilities, strong areas and traits that make us unique. Our family benefits from them, even if they do not acknowledge it and in ways they are unable to understand. When we try to find the positive in negative things, let us take a clue from this story by an unknown author:

> There once was an oyster whose story I tell.
> Who found that sand had got under his shell.
> Just one little grain, but it gave him much pain.
> For oysters have feelings although they're so plain.
>
> Now, did he berate the workings of fate,
> which had let him to such a deplorable state?
> Did he curse out the government, call for an election?
> No, as he lay on the shelf, he said to himself:
> 'If I cannot remove it, I'll try to improve it.'
>
> So the years rolled by as the years always do,
> and he came to his ultimate destiny, stew.
> And this small grain of sand which had bothered him so,
> was a beautiful pearl, all richly aglow.
>
> Now this tale has a moral, for isn't it grand,
> what an oyster can do with a morsel of sand?

> What couldn't we do if we'd only begin,
> with all the things that get under our skin.

There is another pearl that seems like it is given to us by Mary. In the words of Elihu Burritt:

> I would say to all: Use your gentlest voice at home. Watch it day by day as a pearl of great price; for it will be worth more to you in days to come than the best pearl hid in the sea. A kind voice is joy, like a lark's song, to a hearth at home. Train it to sweet tones now, and it will keep in tune through life.

Fr Léonce de Grandmaison composed this prayer to Our Lady:

Holy Mary, Mother of God, preserve in me the heart of a child, pure and transparent as a spring. Obtain for me a simple heart that does not brood over sorrows; a heart generous in giving itself, quick to feel compassion, a faithful, generous heart that forgets no favor and holds no grudge. Give me a humble, gentle heart loving without asking any return, a great indomitable heart that no ingratitude can close, no indifference can weary. A heart tortured by its desire for the glory of Jesus Christ, pierced by his love, with a wound that will heal only in heaven. Amen.

Down through the long pages of history, Christians have shown a deep love and a reverence for the mother of Jesus. This makes sense. No one has honored her more than God who chose her to be the mother of his son. Hymns have been sung in her honor, multitudes have gone on pilgrimages to her shrines. Her pictures and statues are found in humble homes, small chapels, suburban Churches, and great basilicas where her son is worshipped. More importantly she is, after Jesus, the embodiment of everything that is beautiful, good, pure, and holy in creation. Mary is the best example

of eternal motherhood and noble womanhood. However, her primary purpose is to lead everyone to her
son. Long ago, Mary stood alone. She was the first
woman to believe in Jesus. Since then her influence has
been phenomenal.

A Steadfast Guide

Throughout the course of history Mary has inspired
more men and women than any other woman who ever
lived. Like countless women before us, women of today
are invited to follow Mary. Women are icons of change
when they bring the light of Christ to a society darkened
by sin. By imitating Mary, mystic women instill into
society the most important change agent it needs—
holiness. These women resemble small flames of light
in the dark night of degrading TV programs, demeaning entertainment, corrupting fashions, foul language,
adoration of celebrities and shady business practices.
Encouraged by, and following Mary's banner of love,
mystic women sacrifice for their families, those less
fortunate and those in crisis situations. This counteracts
the current 'every man for himself' mentality. Mystic
women are, and teach others to be, polite and courteous,
especially to people with angry retorts and crude
comebacks. 'Have a blessed day' has more integrity
than its more common and very frayed counterpart. A
difference of opinion is expressed civilly, thereby
returning an element of class to heated discussions.
Mystic women stand tall and straight in the face of
opposition. They are not afraid to bring chivalry to
society by setting limits on public behavior, drawing
forth the good that is in others, defending the helpless
among us, dressing with dignity, speaking respectfully

and maintaining sturdy and sound values. Like the lady of their homesteads, mystic women are gallant and forthright, in a lady like way. They know little acts of love offered to Jesus will bring people entrenched in sin back to God. They never underestimate the grace of God at work in difficult situations, even when the graces cannot be perceived.

In peaceful times when our steps are firm and our lives are easy, and in fearful times when our steps are unsteady in desert sand, we hold on to God alone. Then we find a rich harvest in our joy or in our sorrow. With Mary as our guide we experience exquisite wonder, profound peace and unspeakable graces. As we strive to stand by Mary, we know she stands by us with motherly closeness. She is there during the happy days and the hard days that pass in our lives. She supports our hesitant steps with loving care as we travel the path her son has left for us. As we walk forward, we sing her minor litany:

> Ladder by which we climb to the sublime.
> Star by whose bright light we brave the night.
> Mirror in which we see eternity.
> Key that will unlock the house on the rock.
> Tower by which we stand, strong in a strange land.
> Rose in whose rustling stirred the eternal word.
> Lady of quietness.
> Queen of mysteries.
> Remember us.

Notes

1   St Thomas, *Summa Theologiae* I, q. 25, a. 6.
2   Flower of Carmel (*Flos Carmeli*) has been used, since 1663, by
     the Carmelites as the sequence for the Feast of Our Lady of
     Mount Carmel. Its composition is ascribed to St Simon Stock
     (circa 1165–1265).
3   Sister Mary Ada CSJ, 'Limbo'.

3

GIVE US THIS DAY

'Bless us O Lord, and these thy gifts, which we are about to receive from thy bounty' is a common family prayer heard at the table before meals. If the family is large a revision might be: 'In the name of the Father and of the Son and of the Holy Ghost, whoever eats the fastest gets the most.' A French prayer is lovely in its simplicity: 'For this good food and joy renewed, we praise your name O Lord.' Whatever the before meal prayer, thanksgiving is offered for the gifts on the table and the gifts of the day. What a privilege it is to be life long learners in the art of prayer.

Who is the person who has helped countless numbers of people grow in this art of prayer? Teresa Sánchez de Cepeda Ávila y Ahumada, also known as Teresa de Jesus or Saint Teresa of Avila. She was a Spanish Carmelite nun, in sixteenth century Spain, who fashioned in the Church a new expression of Carmelite life. She lived after the Council of Trent, in times much like our own. She restored the primitive rule of Carmel which had been relaxed, and infused into it a deeper spirit of prayer. She founded the monastery of St Joseph in Avila, which was a small group of cloistered nuns dedicated to a life of prayer, poverty, solitude, community and sisterly charity. During her lifetime she established seventeen monasteries of nuns, and with John of the Cross, restored the

primitive rule in new houses of Carmelite friars in
Spain. Her foundations of nuns and friars became a
separate province of the Carmelite Order before she
died in 1587. Teresa was charming, vivacious, and
determined. She had common sense, a warm personality, dear friends, a delightful sense of humor and
sound intelligence. She experienced the highest forms
of prayer and wrote about them in the book, which she
considered her best work: *The Interior Castle*. It is
unequaled in Christian literature, and remains a spiritual classic to this day. Teresa is a guide for all who
love life and are called to the heroicity of daily duty.
She shows us that holiness and wholesomeness are
companions on the road to sanctity. Teresa challenges
us to follow her to the heights. She teaches us that there
is no better way to God than the way of prayer.

Heartbeat of the Soul

As we move forward on the spiritual journey, there is
a mystery and wonder in prayer that is ever rediscovered. It is an adventure, for we never know where it
will lead us. Indeed, prayer is the key that opens us up
to God's mystery. One definition of prayer is a movement of the heart toward God. We can talk to God
about our ups and downs, joys and sorrows, bright
lights, dark nights and anything in between. He knows
our needs and we will get what we need when we need
it. Prayer is the mainstay of our kith, kin, hearth and
home. All that we do in everyday life can be weighted
and considered before God. All that comes to us in
time can be a bridge to eternity.

Jesus is always available to listen to us. We open
our hearts and lay before him our deepest thoughts.

He lets us know what is essential and what is not, what is on the surface and what has depth, what is true and what is false. Jesus said 'Come to me all you who labor and are burdened and I shall refresh you.' We sit at his feet and drink from the wisdom that flows from his heart. Jesus' heart symbolizes his immense and all consuming love for humanity. No one is left out. Jesus invites us to take refuge in his heart. As we enter into the depths of this heart, we are overwhelmed with mercy. We feel safe, free and loved. We are safe because Jesus' heart is a sanctuary of love. We are free from all that causes us undue worry and stress. We are loved in a way we never experienced before. To dwell in the heart of Christ is to simply dwell in his goodness and love. We take to heart the words of Elizabeth Anne Vanek: 'Crawl into the wounded heart of God and there find mercy. Hide, take refuge from all that bounds you into the dust; those in pursuit draw close, itching to tear you from limb to limb, frantic for your blood. Crawl in deeper: there, in the heart's core, carve a place of safety where none dare follow; secure at last, cast off fear and gaze instead on the One who weeps for you and for the world. Let heart speak to heart tenderly.'

What do we learn in the sanctuary of Jesus' heart? The principles that guide what we say and do must come from the teachings of Jesus. The primary way we understand and implement them is by a fervent prayer life. We seek Christ in everything that happens to us, and his goodness and love gives us strength and hope. Jesus' heart is pierced by our sins, yet it continues to beat for our salvation. Heart of Jesus, wherein are all the treasures of wisdom and knowledge, have mercy on us.

Jesus poured out love from his heart in his miracles, in the reconciliation of sinners, in his compassionate actions, in the institution of the Eucharist and in his passion and death. After Jesus died a solider pierced his side with a lance. Water and blood flowed from that wound. The water represented baptism, and the blood represented the Eucharist. These were the signs of life and love through which the Church was born. The Church in turn, continues to give life and love to the faithful which continues to this day. Peter Chrysologus describes the Church as a garden that extends all over the world:

> Christ became all things in order to restore all of us in himself. The man Christ received the mustard seed which represents the kingdom of God; as man he received it, though as God he had always possessed it. He sowed it in his garden, that is in his bride, the Church. The Church is a garden extending over the whole world, tilled by the plough of the gospel, fenced in by stakes of doctrine and discipline, cleared of every harmful weed by the labor of the apostles, fragrant and lovely with perennial flowers: virgins' lilies and martyrs' roses, set amid the pleasant verdure of all who bear witness to Christ and the tender plants of all who have faith in him.
>
> Such then is the mustard seed which Christ sowed in his garden. When he promised a kingdom to the patriarchs the seed took root in them; with the prophets it sprang up, with the apostles it grew tall, in the Church it became a great tree putting forth innumerable branches laden with gifts. And now you too must take the wings of the psalmist's dove, gleaming gold in

the rays of divine sunlight, and fly to reap for
ever among those sturdy, fruitful branches. No
snares are set to trap you there; fly off, then, with
confidence and dwell securely in its shelter.[1]

Prayer is the life line we must have to remain faithful
to our commitments and continue our journey. We
cling to it no matter how busy we may be. When we
are faithful to daily reflective prayer, our other duties
and responsibilities fall into place. Prayer changes
things. It gives us the push we need to get things done.
We maintain a positive outlook when negativity
surrounds us. The fruit of our prayer is the love we
bring to our families and work place, to our parish and
social activities.

Sometimes we are like airline pilots flying at night
or through a storm. They depend on radar contact with
the control tower to stay on course. Pilots are able to
arrive at the destination without seeing the way ahead.
As Christians we make our way through our dark
nights of pain and storms of trials by using prayer as
a radar of sorts. In times when we feel we are going
off course, or when we cannot see what lies ahead, we
maintain contact with God, and things come out all
right in the end. The only way we are able to keep
moving in darkness and storms is by truly believing
that God is in control. Teresa of Avila tells us that
physical strength and stamina are not necessary to
move forward in prayer. All God asks of us is that we
do the best we can with what we have, and leave the
rest to him. To love God greatly during rough times
has more worth than to love him in a small way during
times when things are going smoothly. Sometimes we
can be so tired that we fall asleep during our daily
prayer time. Not to worry. We are in good company.

Therese of Lisieux fell asleep frequently while at prayer with her sisters in the choir. She noted that just as parents love their children as much while they are asleep as while they are awake, so God loved her even though she often slept during the time for prayers. She gives us a lovely definition of prayer: 'Prayer means a launching out of the heart towards God; it means lifting up one's eyes, quite simply, to heaven, a cry of grateful love, from the crest of joy or the trough of despair; it's a vast, supernatural force that opens out my heart and binds me close to Jesus.'

Therese also lets us know how God cares for each person as if that person was the only one he created. God loves those who resemble small, fragile lilies of the field as much as he loves those who resemble large and sturdy oak trees. 'I understood too that the love of our Lord is revealed in the simplest soul who offers no resistance to his grace as well as in the most sublime soul. In fact, since the essence of love is humility, if all souls were like those of the learned saints who have illuminated the Church by the light of their teaching, it would seem as if God would not have very far to descend in coming to their hearts. But he has created the baby who knows nothing and whose only utterance is a feeble cry; he has created people who have only the law of nature to guide them; and it is their hearts that he deigns to come down to, those are his flowers of the field whose simplicity delights him. In coming down in that way the good God proves his infinite greatness. Just as the sun shines at the same time on cedar trees and on each little flower as if it was the only one on earth, so our Lord takes special care of each soul as if it was his only care.'

An Ongoing Adventure

Early in our prayer quest, like most good things, prayer is comforting and sweet. It makes us feel good. Like a soft kitten or a box of chocolates. This surface sentiment makes our eyes sparkle with happiness and our hearts flutter with delight. Everything is wonderful and sweet. We find much enjoyment when we pray. We treasure it, but like all honeymoons in life, the delights in prayer do not last.

Eventually this 'honeymoon prayer' fades into the reality of work a day prayer. We find that prayer, like love, is not dependent on emotions, sentiment or whim. Although personal feelings are a part of prayer, they are largely irrelevant. They may help us or hinder us. However, the object of prayer is not to please ourselves, but to please God. Prayer is the time we take after we answer the door on which God knocks. It is up to us to let him in so that he can be with us. He may speak to us; but even if he does not, we are in his company. We ponder and cherish God in the sanctuary home of our hearts. When it is more a matter of loving than a matter of thinking or feeling, our prayer is more communion than communication.

As we become more sensitive to God, we are more aware of his presence within us and more open to his word and action. When this happens, the roughness of our faults and sins are slowly sanded down and a delicate spiritual design emerges. If we are assiduous daily pray-ers, prayer becomes a mirror that reflects who we are. We are startled at what we see, but we know that the way to prove the validity of our prayer is to improve our lives. If our prayer is less than satisfactory, there is usually something in our lives that needs to be upgraded. The way we deal with issues in our lives leaves a residue that manifests itself in our prayer. We would like to be the type of person we imagine ourselves to be when we pray. However, negative memories, harsh words and irresponsible actions play back during prayer. Our foolish laughter, silly behavior and misguided thoughts disturb us. When this happens, we must switch our thought mode to God. Ruminating on negative things in our lives moves us away from God.

A mind focused on God keeps distractions at a minimum. It also gives us the energy to keep working in order to diminish the division between who we are and who we want to be. Actively seeking the will of God gives our lives a positive and loving energy. How we respond to his will, which is love, is reflected in how we respond to the question: What value does this have in the light of eternity? Mindful of our own weakness, we repeatedly call to God for assistance. 'God, come to my assistance' is a prayer that extends far beyond the beginning of the Liturgy of the Hours. By keeping God in mind we add a spiritual dimension to our actions. A balanced relationship between the quality of our prayer and the spiritual content of our actions is apparent to others. Angry outbursts are toned down. The methods we use to enhance our egos are rarely used. Snappy retorts that hurt others are no longer needed as a defense and fall by the wayside. The artificial areas of our lives are identified and diminished. Prayer unveils our subconscious motivations. We think we live for God but find who we really serve. The way we live indicates the quality of our prayer. When we actively seek the will of God there is no desire to fabricate, repress, deny or rationalize. We experience the truth of our being: we know we are sinners. Sin weakens our prayer and habitual serious sin deadens it. Striving to lead a God centered life moves us toward a more profound experience of prayer which, like life, is profound mystery.

Prayer can range from the deeply muddled to the highly mystical. Whatever the experience, we remain faithful to prayer. Our fidelity to prayer leads to a change in how we respond to various aspects of our daily lives. If we think we pray well and continue to exhibit certain negative behaviors, we are fools. There are occult traits that have the capacity to deplete the potency of prayer. A spiritual selfishness and complacency are the most hidden of traits. Frequently voicing our opinion, collecting things that enhance our spiritual self-image or a fixation on success focus on whom? The same goes for passionate likes and dislikes and frequent episodes of exhaustion or excitement. How easily our gaze can move from the life of the God man to the life of the god me. If our prayer is true, our way of thinking, talking and acting will change toward the good. An authentic focus on Jesus helps us to be more aware of what is good, wise, beautiful and true in our lives. In the Triune God centered space within our hearts, we find nourishment that feeds our decision making capacities with accurate information that guards and guides us toward what is holy.

Practical Application

Spiritual growth is rarely achieved by a multiplicity of prayers. It is easy to mindlessly recite words, which can sometimes be rather hypnotizing. As our intimacy with Jesus deepens, our personal devotions are simplified. A wide assortment of devotional practices may help us at one stage of our life, but hinder our growth as we advance toward greater intimacy with God. Indeed, we can almost be buried under the weight of many vocal prayers or private devotions. Advanced prayer is not a myriad of personal devotions or heavenly sensations. It is much more basic. Jesus is God's word to us. Instead of saying an inordinate number of prayers we need only to look at him. This may not take hours of our time or result in good feelings. We make a decision to give our attention to God, and do not concern ourselves about feelings or using our imagination. How well we know that extreme emotions or feelings are dangerous, spiritually and otherwise. Strong emotions or feelings, or the experience of signs and wonders, or the anticipation of miracles are dangerous because the imagination can play tricks or run away with us. A mind can be deceiving. How many times has it lead us astray? How often do we think things are worse than they actually are, or engage in unrestrained fantasy? How often are we unusually curious, make ungrounded assumptions or discuss things without reaching a conclusion based on God's truth? When we hear the voice of God, how do we know it is not an echo of our ego? Referring to the misuse of our imagination, Teresa of Avila said: 'The imagination is the fool of the house.' That is something to think about. We need to maintain control of our imagination. Then we will remain faithful to the still small voice of God that leads us into the depths of prayer without our knowing it. Prayer is not sweet imaginings that delight our spiritual appetite, but a daily spiritual hunger that, if not satisfied, causes an unexplainable void within us.

From time to time, we experience a wordless wonder of God that is beyond intelligence, imagination or
emotion. This deeper state of prayer is like a quiet
awareness of a sacred twilight filled with the subtle
beauty of God. We cannot see clearly nor are we unable
to see. The words of Jesus 'Abide in my love' rest in
our hearts. Our thoughts are suspended, replaced by
an indescribable awe. We are lost in God's exquisite
light. Our knowledge of God can be compared to
someone standing at the edge of an ocean at midnight
trying to see across it with the light from a lantern.
What we know about God with our little light is just
right for us.

> Jesus, thou joy of loving hearts,
> Thou fount of life, thou light of men,
> From the best bliss that earth imparts,
> We turn unfilled to thee again.

> Thy truth unchanged hath ever stood;
> Thou savest those who on thee call;
> To them that seek thee, thou art good,
> To them that find thee, all in all.

> We taste thee, O thou living bread,
> And long to feast upon thee still;
> We drink of thee the Fountainhead,
> And thirst, our souls from thee to fill.

> Our restless spirits yearn for thee,
> Where'er our changeful lot is cast;
> Glad, when thy gracious smile we see,
> Blest, when our faith can hold thee fast.

> O Jesus, ever with us stay
> Make all our moments calm and bright;
> Chase the night of sin away;
> Shed o'er the world thy holy light.[2]

We need Jesus every minute of the day. He helps us move along in mystery and in trust. Without him the challenges of the day would cause us to flee in fear and trembling. Jesus is our strength, hope and consolation. Without him nothing would make sense.

Often we speak to him in short prayers from our hearts. It seems like 'Jesus help me,' is the most common short prayer. We are welcome to ask for his help with the insignificant things nobody knows are troubling to us. It is always followed by 'Thank you, Lord.' 'Jesus, I love you,' gives our minds and hearts a lift. 'All for Jesus,' gives new meaning to unpleasant or difficult duties. In these short prayers of the moment there is a genuine connection with God. We affirm our conviction that Jesus is here for us and that we live in his presence. Just a word or two expresses our petition, gratitude or love to the Triune God. Indeed, we are perpetual students in the school of prayer and we never stop learning about this fine art.

John of the Cross reminds us that God is looking for us more eagerly than we are looking for him. In the depths of prayer we find that everything finite is a stepping stone to, and a reminder of, the infinite. Our prayer interpretations seem irrelevant when they are compared with the real fruit of prayer. The true fruit of prayer is the will of God manifested in and lived by us. This happens, in part, by positive changes in our personalities and demeanor. Indeed, we quietly pray for others, and we who pray for others become convinced of our own need for reform. Personal reform changes how we look at things and people. We no longer judge a book by its cover. We no longer judge people by how they look. We are reminded of the porcupine's prayer: 'Lord let them know my protection is also my insulation. Help them to look beyond my appearance. I am truly soft underneath.' Edith Stein wrote a little poem: 'Judge not lest you be judged in turn, appearances cloud our view. We guess at the truth, but only learn God alone knows what is true.'

By Grace Refined

Augustine's words 'Noverim Te, noverim me', (May I know you, may I know myself), are a cry of the heart that brings us to the center of our individuality.[3] Here we focus on our real priorities. We passed through the clamor of power games, glamour, consumerism and other parasitical fleeting and wounding entities that absorb time and energy. True knowledge of ourselves gives us a focus that captures and holds our attention on God and his goodness in the world. Divine love creates and sustains all things in good order. Love draws everything to itself. As we experience new depths of love, we are more aware of God working in and through his creation. To accept the values found in a life of holiness is to accept a vision that sees beyond current situations. Such is the vision of the mystic. When we think clearly and do rightly, we sustain life beyond ourselves and our time slot in history. We are windows that let the light of God's life and love shine through us into our environments. Therein lies the beauty of holiness. We see what is essential. Life is lived in grace rather than learned like an academic lesson. Wisdom and grace help us to choose that which is soul worthy, and therefore life giving.

Wisdom fashioned in the heart tells us that we need determination to persevere in prayer. In spite of difficulty and discouragement, we press onward in our prayer quest and work at cultivating sound virtues. Some virtues go against our grain, and take time to formulate. A result of our perseverance in prayer is a deeper wisdom about our shortcomings. Teresa of Avila tells us that as we progress toward God there comes a time when the sense of our own sins as set against the purity, majesty and love of God, becomes an unbearable burden. We may think we are no better than we were last year, but the reality is that our focus is sharper and our shortcomings clearer. We may not notice any change, but God does. Because we have grown closer to God, the differences between him and us are more acute. The harmless attitudes and behavior we might have found to be praiseworthy, now are seen as vain, selfish and even sinful. In the light of greater faith we see ourselves as we are in God's sight. This spurs us into action because it is a powerful incentive to grow in virtue. An increase in wisdom should be distressing enough for us to do something about it. A great confidence in God's love and mercy will help us overcome our faults.

A noble purpose in life is fidelity to the duties of the present moment. We reflect upon Jesus' presence in our hearts and bring his presence to practical application in our daily activities. We reflect on the God of today, the God of the present, not the God of yesterday or tomorrow. What does God want of us today? Edith Stein counsels:

> God is there... and can give us in a single instant exactly what we need. Then the rest of the day can take its course, under the same effort and strain, perhaps, but in peace. And when night comes, and you look back over the day and see how fragmentary everything has been, and how

> much you planned that has gone undone, and
> all the reasons you have to be embarrassed and
> ashamed, just take everything exactly as it is, put
> it in God's hands and leave it with him. Then
> you will be able to rest in him—really rest—and
> start the next day as a new life.

Such an orientation shows us how each day is precious and teaches us to be fully present in the moment. Even in times when our families experience financial trouble, acute or chronic illness, psychological dysfunction, betrayal of friends, terrorizing events or the death of a loved one, deep underneath the surface tension we know God is in control.

In the Hands of God

Authentic belief in 'give us this day our daily bread' is a spiritually mature conviction that God's Providence will provide us with what we need. This does not mean we should max out our credit cards, live for the pleasures of the moment, avoid making future plans or establishing retirement accounts, or exist outside the realm of common sense. If we trust in God's goodness we do not obsess about negatives that the future may hold or inordinately stockpile provisions. Believing in the Providence of God consists of living simply, not worrying, conserving our resources, respecting all of God's creation, appreciating what we have, giving what we do not need to the less fortunate, and not thinking that the grass is greener on the other side of the fence. We are content with our lot in life and are faithful in the simplicity of God's will today. We need not seek asceticism or struggles for they are mapped out for us. We recognize how often we live

between a fragile trust and a sad kind of aloneness. A
spiritual sobriety tells us great rivers of beauty have
undercurrents of sadness. Reflections of light are in
the darkness of pain. We just ask for the strength to
live in harmony and peaceful joy, and from this we
find that daily bread not only means material things
but also unexpected surprises that dot our days: a look
of tenderness, a word of encouragement, a happy
surprise in the mail or a chance meeting with a friend.

If we are obedient to the Word day by day unto our
death, we are doing what God asks of us. This four-
teenth century hymn, whose author is unknown, helps
us keep Christ close at hand:

> Soul of Christ, sanctify me.
> Body of Christ, save me.
> Water from the side of Christ, wash me.
> Passion of Christ, strengthen me.
> O good Jesus, hear me.
> Within thy wounds hide me.
> Suffer me not to be separated from thee.
> From the malignant enemy defend me.
> In the hour of my death, call me.
> And bid me come to thee,
> that, with thy saints, I may praise thee
> forever and ever. Amen.[4]

What can we do to strengthen the spiritual bonds in
our family? Praying together each day is most important. Sharing spiritual stepping stones at a Sunday
night family gathering once a month is helpful. The
room is dark and a candle is lit for each family member. Then each person could respond to a few of the
following: What are my most treasured bible stories?
What are my spiritual strengths and weaknesses?
What are my special devotions, best loved hymns and

holydays? How do I see God? What are my favorite prayers and places to pray? What are the ways I receive and share God's love? When are the times I thought God had forgotten me? How would I describe the times when God seems very close? Tell about the times when my faith became real for me? What events/persons have influenced my spiritual journey? How have unexpected people manifested the humanity of Jesus to me? What are God's most beautiful created gifts? What are the special moments on my spiritual journey? How do I live out the gospel? What are the ways I see the mystery of God in my daily life? Sketch and explain my spiritual symbol and personal seal. How has Jesus changed my life? What are my spiritual thoughts for posterity?

Blaise Pascal once said 'The serene beauty of a holy life is the most powerful influence in the world next to the power of God.' All of us are called to the beauty of holiness, no matter in what conditions of life we live. The quest for holiness is available in all the elements of our days, not just in the religious things we do. It is inclusive and all embracing. The two major attributes of sanctity are thinking positive and living Jesus. We are all beloved children of a loving God and we live this statement by our words and deeds. Helder Camara tells us:

> There is no single definition of holiness, there are dozens, hundreds. But there is one I am particularly fond of: being holy means getting up immediately every time you fall, with humility and joy. It doesn't mean never falling into sin. It means being able to say 'Yes, Lord, I have fallen a thousand times. But thanks to you I have gotten up a thousand and one times.' That's all. I like thinking about that.

Therefore, holiness helps us to embrace and integrate our own and our family's wounds. By doing this, wounds become experiences for learning, strengthening and growing rather than objects for fragmentation, regression or obsession. Holiness is present in the quality of love that is shown in the home and is the foundation of the family's spirituality. In other words, holiness is love in action: Rising at three in the morning to tend to a child's needs, teaching a child how to ride a bike, preparing food for a family barbeque or playing a game of checkers with one's spouse. Teenagers manifest holiness when they change their baby brother's or sister's diapers without complaint, fold the laundry, iron clothes well, or wash the cars without being asked to do so. Holiness motivates us to open up wider and thereby to love more deeply. It always calls forth new life in ourselves and in those we serve.

We learn to love when we are stretched and humbled by the tensions and demands of our family. Irritations and frustrations give us the opportunity to avoid negative mind tapes and to strive to love without conditions. It is so easy to see the faults in other people. We realize that a downbeat, gloomy pattern of thinking leads to a chronic heavy heart, troubled mind and dark soul. It does not allow for empathy, faith, unity and love. Who needs someone who is always writing new verses to the ballad of the wet blanket? If we believe in God's merciful love for us, we will be channels of hope for others. To do this, our love must sustain, uplift and invite trust. Love focuses on the positives in people and optimism in life. We concentrate on the delightful idiosyncrasies, kind acts, fine qualities and 'good news' of people. A person is not a maze of problems to be solved, but rather an unfolding mystery to be discovered, no matter how long we have known him or her. What happens when we are kind to people who irritate us the most? Love rubs off our rough edges and smoothes theirs too. Love gives us the grace to be caring in trying situations. Micah 6:8 tells us how to live together peacefully. We do so by acting justly, loving tenderly and walking humbly with our God.

Christ has too much beauty and goodness for the human heart to bear. He is the greatest of lovers and we can only listen and surrender to him. He energizes our actions, consecrates our pain and helps us to accept the night, and whatever it brings, with trust. We know to whom we belong and who we are. Therese of Lisieux sums it up very beautifully for us: 'Everything is grace. Everything is the direct effect of our Father's love... because everything is God's gift. Whatever be the character of life or its unexpected events—to the heart that loves, all is well.'

> Lord of all pots, pans and needs
> Since I've little time to do great things
> Or watch late in the night with thee
> There is no time for long dreams at dawn
> Or extensive pleads at heaven's gate
> Make me a saint by getting meals
> And washing up the many plates
> Although I must have Martha's hands
> Give Mary's heart to me
> And when I clean the children's shoes
> Thy sandals, Lord, I see
> I think of how they trod the earth
> Whenever I scrub the floor
> Accept this meditation Lord
> I've not much energy for more
> Warm all my kitchen with thy love
> And fill it with thy peace

Forgive me all my worrying
And make my grumbles cease
Thou who generously gave men food
At home or by the sea
Accept the service that I do
I do it all for thee.[5]

Notes

[1]   St Peter Chrysologus, *Homily 98* in *PL* 52, 475–476.

[2]   Bernard of Clairvaux (twelfth century), *Jesu dulcis memoria*;
      translated from Latin into English by Ray Palmer, 1858, in his
      Poetical Works (New York: 1876).

[3]   St Augustine, *Soliloquiorum Liber* II, I,1.

[4]   This well known Catholic prayer dates back to the early
      fourteenth century and was possibly written by Pope John XXII.

[5]   A poem written by a nineteen-year-old girl in domestic
      service in England.

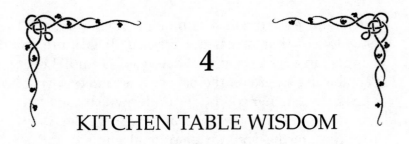

4

KITCHEN TABLE WISDOM

There is an old saying that goes like this: Yes, it is true that God created man before woman, but doesn't one always create a rough draft before the final masterpiece?

Well, final masterpieces are never quite understood and always retain an element of mystery. In order to understand women as mystics, we need to be aware of, and grow in, the mystery of God. We as women, by living up to our divine calling, reflect the love of God as no other. Being a woman is a great privilege. Women are endowed with splendid gifts, evident in a contemplative awareness which is tender, compassionate and strong. Sadly, a good number of women misuse, or are unaware of, their contemplative nature. Such a contemplative oriented maternal instinct is a reflection of the tenderness of God and we should honor it as such.

The book of Genesis tells us that woman was created from the rib of man. Therefore, she was not made to be above him or below him. She came from his side, to be by his side as an equal with him. She is to be protected by his physical strength and he is to be protected by her inner strength. She is near his heart to be beloved by him and he is in her heart to be singularly cherished by her. A long life together is not the only way in which a man and a woman come to understand each other. It is more in loving, than in being loved, that hearts are blessed. It is more in giving, than in receiving, that deep joy is found. Love is an abiding desire on the part of husband and wife to produce together conditions under which each can be and express his or her real self. Together they produce a fertile soil, an emotional climate and a spiritual environment in which each can flourish in a much more superior way than in what either could achieve alone. True nobility comes from a gentle presence, and it is this gentle presence that quells the silly, superficial, flighty, rebellious tempests that are part and parcel of life.

Family is the loom on which we weave our love. Warp meets weft in the home. If we ever have exalted opinions of ourselves, these imaginings come crashing down when we are with family. In family feasts, fasts and ordinary times we find how far we still have to go and what we need to improve ourselves. After all, who is best at irritating us? Family members can grate on us like rough sandpaper or soothe us like sweet balm. When they are like sandpaper we look beneath the surface emotion. Rage, sarcasm, anger or criticism can mask fear. Many times a personal attack is a cry for help. A harsh or vicious question can show that the person who asked it is in need of assistance. Indeed, each person with whom we live is a mystery that must be ever rediscovered, slowly, reverently, carefully, tenderly and painfully and is still never to be discovered completely.

There is an unusual assortment of people in the convent as well as in the home. When Therese of Lisieux was in Carmel she helped an old, crotchety nun to walk along the corridors. All Therese received were complaints: 'You move too fast.' Therese slowed down. 'Well, come on, now you are too slow.' Therese walked a bit faster. 'I don't feel your hand, you let go of me and I'm going to fall.' Therese tightened her grasp. 'I was right when I said you were too young to help me.' Her complaints seemed endless. Therese took it all in stride and managed with a smile. There was another sister who rubbed Therese the wrong way. Instead of avoiding her, when Therese saw her, she gave her a lovely smile. This caused the sister to ask 'Sister Therese of the Child Jesus, would you tell me what attracts you so much towards me? Every time you look at me I see you smile.' Therese responded that she smiled because she was happy to see her. (She did not tell her that this was from a spiritual standpoint.) Therese was very aware of Christ hidden in the souls of her sisters. This was part of her little way to spiritual maturity.

Who was Therese of Lisieux, commonly called the Little Flower? Therese Martin was born in France, the ninth child of Louis and Zelie Martin. Four of the Martin's children died before they reached their fifth year. When Therese was four and a half, Zelie, an exquisite lace maker and an exceptional mother, died from breast cancer. This had a profound effect on Therese.

As a child Therese was affectionate, stubborn, mischievous, intelligent, precocious, and was prone to temper tantrums when things did not go her way. Shortly after his wife's death, Louis, now a single parent, moved his family to Lisieux. The girls named their new home Les Buissonnets, which means little thickets or bushes. It was a comfortable, charming, roomy house, with expansive lawns, trees, and a

garden outside. Therese attended school at a Benedic-
tine abbey as a day boarder. This was the saddest
period of her life. She spent five years there and after
that difficult time was tutored privately. Her home life
was devout, sheltered and filled with love and joy.

Therese's two older sisters, Pauline and Marie,
entered the Carmel of Lisieux. After some painful trials
at age fifteen, Therese did the same. Later on Celine
joined her three sisters and Leone entered the Visita-
tion convent at Caen. Therese spent the last nine years
of her life in Carmel. She was known to be a good nun,
but there was nothing externally remarkable about her.
She worked in the sacristy, cleaned the dining room,
wrote plays and poetry, painted pictures, instructed
novices and participated in the prayer life of the sisters.

When her sister Pauline was prioress, she asked
Therese to write her autobiography. *The Story of a Soul*
has been translated into some forty languages and has
sold millions of copies. It remains popular today as a
sure guide to holiness for anyone who wants to love
Jesus wholeheartedly.

Therese contracted tuberculosis, and suffered im-
mensely in body and soul during the last year and a
half of her life. She was born into eternal life on
September 30, 1897, at the age of twenty-four. Therese
spends her heaven doing good upon earth, as she
promised she would.

When Therese worked in the sacristy, one of her
favorite duties was to place communion hosts in the
ciborium before Mass. Today, there are still monasteries of contemplative nuns that prepare, bake and
distribute communion hosts to parishes in their area.
The words of the preparatory prayers at the beginning
of the Liturgy of the Eucharist have deep meaning:

'Blessed are you, Lord God of all creation, for through your goodness we have received the bread we offer you: fruit of the earth and work of human hands, it will become for us the bread of life.' The altar is sometimes called the table of the Lord. At this table, simple bread becomes the body of Christ; and wine, fruit of the vine and also the work of human hands, becomes the blood of Christ. This is the greatest and most unfathomable mystery on the earth! While sitting at our kitchen table, in an atmosphere of peace and quiet, we would do well to dwell on the words of this hymn:

> O Lord, with wondrous mystery
> You take our bread and wine.
> And make of these two humble things,
> Yourself, our Lord divine.
> Our wheat and drink become our light,
> Our altar bears your awesome might;
> O Lord, we thank you for the gift
> That lies before our sight.
>
> You are the same our Christ and Lord,
> Who blessed the supper room;
> You are the God who died and rose
> Triumphant from the tomb.
> This bread bears your divinity,
> The cup contains infinity;
> The myst'ry fills our souls with love,
> O holy majesty.[1]

A kitchen table can be used for many things. On a higher level it can be a place to listen with the ears of the heart, look with the eyes of the soul, and speak with the tongue of the wise. The superficial use of words and actions are laid aside and replaced by an attentive presence. Thoughts filter gently through the heart and cause an individual to be more aware of his or her own heart. Women can bring out what is best in others (or what is worst in others). However, times around the kitchen table call out for our best. The table can be a place for support, comfort, assistance and prayer. Love calls us to offer encouragement but not in an over zealous way, to console without pity, to teach but not expound, to pray without pietism and to have faith without religiosity. Truth can be revealed in a cold and objective manner, but this is not the way of women. At the kitchen table, truth is a light that shines by our example. It is the light that guides us into action and leadership. We may be slower to reach a conclusion because we keep words and experiences in our hearts in order to understand them more fully. Intuition goes beyond the immediate and apparent need of the moment. To safeguard unity in the family by refraining from quick or sharp responses is to safeguard unity in God's human family. We strive to be receptive to grace and wisdom. Love does not fear going into the depths of suffering or into the heights of joy. A common example here is giving birth. By not fearing life at its depths and heights, women connect the surface world with the grandeur of God.

Strong Bonds

Family strengths develop step by step and require sincere and continuous investments of time, energy, sacrifice, work, forgiveness and love. The following qualities lead to and maintain strong family ties. It is true that these qualities appear to be idealistic expressions, but where would we be if we did not have ideals for which to strive? They offer a clarion call at the top of the mountain which urges us to move forward, in hope and in faith, toward the summit. With every step we take, we remember that the opposite direction does not take strength or endurance. That direction is an easy slide down the slippery slope of negativity and discouragement. We don't need that. Because the traditional family is the sentinel of hope for our society, let us put on our hiking boots and be on our way:

A *religious tradition* keeps a family anchored in God. Daily prayer together is most important. Sound religious practices within a family help it to grow in the right direction, keep circumstances in perspective, provide a sense of purpose to daily activities and give substance to spirituality. It is a very great blessing to be able to live the disciplines, teachings and traditions of the Catholic Christian religion. A religious tradition is the still point that gives the family strength, purpose, reverence, a quality of mystery, transcendence and a firm conviction of God's life and love in their lives. A strong spiritual orientation increases a family's joy and helps them through tragedy. Faith is the glue that holds them together when everything seems to be in ruins.

Cathy is a young girl who loves to pray. She especially likes to pray with her mom, dad, sisters and brothers. Jesus is her dearest friend. Cathy tries to make Jesus happy by being a good girl. She enjoys learning about him and doing what she thinks he would want her to do. Prayer helps to keep her family strong. Cathy is happy when her parents, and other adults, tell stories about well behaved and courteous children they have seen in the market and in other public places. To see a husband, wife and their children, all clean, respectful and neatly dressed, sitting in a pew Sunday after Sunday is a good example that remains in the hearts of other parishioners long after the children have grown up and left home.

Dedication promotes each family member's confidence and welfare through support, loyalty and hope for each other. Dedication is steady and lasting through good times and bad times. It is instilled in the children by parents who deeply love, respect and are faithful to each other despite the vicissitudes of life. The parent's love for each other is the greatest gift they can give to their children.

Susan is a young, attractive single mom with a professional career. Her husband passed away unexpectedly and she is the only support for their five year old son. Because Susan is bright and beautiful, she receives many invitations to social gatherings. However, she turns them down in order to spend time supporting her son and his various activities. She knows the hardships of single parenthood, but would not trade time with her precious boy for the passing thrill of social encounters.

Unselfishness brings happiness that is not related to money, careers or material possessions. It is found in opportunities in which family members can forget themselves, listen, be patient and overlook many things. Unselfishness continually places other family members and their needs first.

A person who gives a little with a smile does more than a person who gives a lot with a frown. We remember and reflect on what Jesus said about the widow and her few coins. She gave from what she had to live on, not from her surplus.

A *team spirit* gathers members together and finds time to do things as a family unit, ranging from regular household chores to playful leisure activities. It inspires each person to graciously extend a helping hand to make work easier or spontaneously play a game to brighten up the day. A team spirit expects no one to be perfect and shares in the joy, pain, happiness or hurt of each member. The ability to pull together as a team builds strength to accept challenges as a part of life.

Ginger was a spitfire and a party girl who loved to dance and have fun, fun, fun. Then Gabrielle, her mother, was diagnosed with lymphoma ... cancer! Ginger did a turn around. She searched the Internet for the best cancer treatment center. She accompanied her mother to doctor appointments and chemotherapy treatments. Gabrielle's illness, and Ginger's response to it, brought mother and daughter closer than ever before. Gabrielle went into remission. Ginger realized the importance of God in her life. Ginger continues to run in marathons for lymphoma and, together with her mom, speaks at and participates in various cancer related activities.

Communication that is honest and open finds time to share ideas, problems, information and thoughts easily and honestly. Communication may range from trivial topics to the deeper issues of life. Quality and quantity time for talking go hand in hand. Open communication airs grievances while they are current and deals with problems one at a time. It disagrees with dignity which excludes criticizing, domineering, blaming, acting the martyr or controlling or manipulating others. Communication calls for prompt forgiveness which is a decision that helps us more than the person we forgive. When we let go of anger, resentment or other negative feelings that hold us captive, it liberates us for authentic communication.

Paul and Patti married and had five children. Both were blessed with an even temperament, most of the time. They learned the fine art of disagreeing without being disagreeable. From time to time they have gotten miffed at each other, but there was no verbal abuse. They realized the futility, absurdity and downward spiral of harsh words, demeaning criticisms, verbal combat, name calling, screaming, cursing and other hurtful manipulations. Although Paul and Patti know how to push each other's buttons, they refrain from doing so. They release their anger and other destructive emotions in positive ways. They also refrain from discussing high tension concerns, problems and issues when they are in a high or low emotional state. They parent as partners and when the children fight among themselves, or pit their parents against each other, Paul and Patti really close ranks and work as a team. They use actions more than words. Paul and Patti have made it a practice to forgive easily, be forthright about how they feel and what they think, speak in low measured tones and try to remain calm and collected. Their behavior has created an environment in which their children feel carefree, secure and appreciated.

Appreciation helps each member to grow and flourish as a unique individual as well as a member of the family. Sincere appreciation promotes family security and solidarity, especially during times of disappointments and setbacks. The overt expression of gratitude heightens awareness of the special contributions of each person, and family members cultivate genuine admiration for one another.

Most all parents know that their children do better work and put forth a greater effort when they receive approval and praise, especially from them. One compliment does more good than a thousand criticisms. To thank children for their little tasks done well brings smiles to their hearts, and subtly reinforces positive behavior.

A *'be not afraid'* perspective views stress as a normal part of life and an opportunity to grow. This positive perspective encourages problem identification and decision making skills, while pursuing realistic goals and sustaining a positive sense of humor about one's self and the family as a whole. A family permeated with hope locates treasures below the surface value of things, finds inspiration and insights in the mundane, and enables whoever they meet to go forward with perseverance.

Lily is an extraordinary minister of Holy Communion in her parish. She brings communion to the homebound, one of whom is a relative of hers. When she visits this relative two other women who live in the house continue to do the dishes and gossip when Lily begins to administer the sacrament. Lily asks them to join her in prayer. They refuse and continue with their chatter and clatter of dishes, without any concern or respect for Jesus in the blessed sacrament. After communion, Lily gently reminds the women that Jesus was present in their home, that this is a beautiful blessing and that prayer is very important in people's lives. Lily is not afraid to speak up about the reverence that is necessary when people are in the presence of the Lord, and on other aspects of her faith.

A *positive attitude* promotes confidence and encourages what is best for the family. It focuses on the good in others and in the circumstances and events of life. Optimism diminishes anxiety and worry during times of travail and expands joy and contentment during pleasant times. Having a positive attitude keeps Easter alive in the family throughout the year.

Luz Maria is a petite, middle-aged single parent with an easy smile and an upbeat disposition. She cleans houses for a living and has elevated her tasks to an art form of which she is proud. One can often hear her humming a happy tune as she works. Children are drawn to her. Adults find peace in her presence. She resembles a ray of sunshine which continues to gleam in the cleanliness and tidiness of the homes where she has finished her work. Her one son is in his twenties, and attends a special education school. He is severely autistic and has frequent seizures. When Luz Maria faces tasks that seem beyond her strength and abilities, she maintains her positive attitude and simply knows that she will get the help she needs because God always comes to her assistance. Luz Maria truly trusts in Divine Providence.

One physician makes it a practice to give this quote by Charles Swindoll to his patients who have cancer:

> The longer I live, the more I realize the impact of attitude on life. Attitude, to me, is more important than facts. It is more important than the past, than education, than money, than circumstances, than failures, than successes, than what other people think or say or do. It is more important than appearances, giftedness or skill. It will make or break a company, a Church, a home. The remarkable thing is we have a choice every day regarding the attitude we will embrace for that day. We cannot change our past … we cannot change the fact that people will act in a certain way. We cannot change the inevitable. The only thing we can do is play on the one string we have, and that is

> our attitude ... I am convinced that life is ten
> percent what happens to me and ninety percent
> how I react to it. And so it is with you ... we are
> in charge of our attitudes.

The happiness in our lives depends on the quality of
our thoughts. A negative thought pattern can be
changed by altering our perception. If we focus on the
good, both in our lives and in the lives of others, our
thoughts will surely have a optimistic orientation.

A Vocation of the Heart

It is often said that being a mother is the most difficult
job there is on this planet. Yet it is so much more than
a job. A Jewish proverb says: 'God could not be
everywhere, so he made mothers.' Therese of Lisieux
adds to this: 'The loveliest masterpiece of the heart of
God is the heart of a mother.' Motherhood is at the
heart of every woman. There is an ingredient of
motherhood in every love that is true and deep.
Christian women are called to be signs of God's love,
tenderness, beauty, dignity and yes, mystery, to the
human race. The more we love God the more we love
others. Our love is not superficial nor is it a detached
benevolence. It is bonded with the strength of inner
values. Yes, it is good to be patriotic, work for social
justice issues or fight for equality. However fine these
causes may be, they need the support of deeply
virtuous, God-centered people in order to endure. The
world is much more than a stage for human conflict.
It is meant to be a home for the whole human family.
The quiet, disciplined, consistent expression of love is
more effective than brilliant reasoning, hard facts, or
erudite debates. Instead of arguing one's point *ad*

infinitum, one takes time for tea and really listens to what the other person has to say. As we learn to love God more, we learn to better share the love he has for others, especially sinners (of whom we include ourselves). When we love God above all else, it gives us the strength and courage to love others without reserve. To love is to serve and our kitchens provide more opportunities to serve than we can count. The next time we stir a huge pot of soup on the stove, we can sing the hymn 'Seek ye first the kingdom of God' and really understand what it means.

All of us have dark memories that affect our outlook. How easily they can surface because of our history, self centeredness, over sensitivity, excessive neediness, or the order in which we want events to happen. We must not deny these dark memories nor frequently dwell on them. God will give us the strength to face them with his light of grace. When dark memories are brought out into the open and faced in a way that turn us around, we will be free to move toward the light of God that illuminates the road to love. Past experiences should be guide posts and not stop signs. Resiliency is a necessary skill in the art of living. The winds of life may bend us, but if we have a resilient spirit they cannot hurt us beyond repair or break us. To courageously straighten up again, after we have been bowed by the winds of defeat, disappointment and suffering is a great test of integrity.

It seems that family members seldom make time for activities that bond them together. What can be done to find time for family interaction? It has been said that children spend about the same amount of time watching TV as they spend in school, and little time talking with their parents. Within this TV mode, their cognitive development, reading and math skills, and creativity suffer. Parents should not use TV viewing as a babysitter or pacifier for their young children. What the children view should be monitored by the parents and limited in time. It would be of great benefit not to watch programs on TV, or play computer games, that are offensive, demeaning, insulting, violent or are otherwise inappropriate. They influence the viewer in many negative ways. Excessive watching of the TV and playing on the computer can easily numb the mind, waste time, avoid communication, and avoid work while contributing to laziness and a sedentary lifestyle. Instant messaging, games, and random surfing on the Internet can be dangerous and time consuming. The predators are lying in wait. Children should be informed and monitored so that they never provide Internet sites with personal information. Such information can easily lead to trouble. Limiting time with electronic media and entertainment will increase time available for family activities.

A sweet memory of adults is remembering stories read to them when they were children by their mother or father. Favorite bedtime stories, especially when they are read on dark and stormy nights, are family treasures. They also help children learn to read. Good reading skills help children learn to handle information and solve problems. A good way to deal with a difficulty is to read a story that has similar circumstances. Books about pioneers or poor folks, inventors or ordinary heroes, gifted students or slow learners, help children to know they are not alone. Reading gives children the ability to see beyond their own circumstances and broadens their view of life. Sharing realistic and positive stories inspire and motivate children to do better in school and aim higher in life.

'Tis a Gift to be Simple

When we prepare food or do other kitchen work for the family, let us remember not to do several things at the same time. In the long run, this does not lend itself to smooth running preparation. Even though multitasking is popular today, and it is common in a business environment, it disrupts our attention and concentration on tasks in the home, especially in the kitchen. Using various kitchen appliances at the same time can be unsafe. Multitasking keeps our mind going in several different directions at once. How often have we burned a special dish because we were distracted by a chatty phone call? It takes high levels of energy to multitask and it cheats us out of doing anything really well. Most of all, in excessive busyness the sacredness of the present moment is lost. By multitasking we do not honor and treasure each task for itself, nor do we work in a contemplative manner.

As we learn to concentrate on and complete one task at a time, we focus on the meaning and value of what we do and who we really are. We begin to let go of the frivolous, superficial and damaging aspects of our lives. How much time do we spend watching the TV, playing on the computer or idly talking on the phone? To live well requires change. Inordinate attachments and pesky appetites delay our mystic journey. Even good things, like favorite prayers and saints, personal devotions, ministries, people or jobs can derail our spiritual journey. They take us off the track if we are addicted to them, if they become an end in themselves or if we see them as magic keys that open the gate of heaven. In what ways are we stuck in the mud of materialism, including spiritual materialism? To live with a relaxed grasp makes change easier. How cluttered our lives become by items such as gimmicks gadgets, fads, unnecessary meetings, self preoccupations, and useless worry. It is bliss to be free of the need for them. How they hinder our spiritual growth and blur our mystical vision!

Simplicity of life deepens the essentials and the beauty of the spiritual journey and drops unneeded accidentals and accretions. True simplicity receives all things as gifts from God. Therese of Lisieux was very fond of snow. In her autobiography she wrote

> I don't know if I've already told you how much I love snow? When I was small, it's whiteness filled me with delight, and one of the greatest pleasures I had was taking a walk under the light snow flakes. Where did this love come from? Perhaps it was because I was a little winter flower, (born Jan 2) and the first adornment with which my eyes beheld nature clothed, was its white mantle. I had always wished that on the day I received the habit, nature would be adorned in white just like me ... the evening before the temperature was so mild I could no longer hope for snow.

On January 10, 1889, right after her clothing day ceremony (reception of the habit which included the white veil and white mantle), Therese embraced her father for the last time and entered the cloister. She tells us:

> My glance was drawn to snow, the monastery garden was white like me! What thoughtfulness

> on the part of Jesus! Anticipating the desires of
> his fiancee, he gave her snow. Snow! ... What
> is certain, though, is that many considered the
> snow on my clothing day as a little miracle and
> the whole town was astonished. Some found I
> had a strange taste, loving snow!

Our God is a God of happy surprises. Often, his voice comes to us through others. If we offer whatever we are doing to God, it will keep us from evil or from getting stuck at a dead end. Many times daily routines can lose their luster. Making dinner can be a chore, especially if the children have been irritable or have taxed our patience during the day. What if we change our focus? We prepare our meal, not for kids who were mischievous imps that kept us in the temptation zone that day, but for beloved muppets who belong to God? If we attempt to see the face of God in the little (and big) ones around us, we will have the ability to make life a forward moving journey. This will banish boredom, mediocrity and stuck in the mud impasses.

Now a journey doesn't mean going somewhere that leads to riches, popularity or exotic countries. A journey orientation is finding wonder and adventure in the small things of life such as looking where the sunbeams from the kitchen window fall, or watching ants walking in single file on the kitchen counter (before you obliterate them). Mystics find adventure where others fail to look and in anything that happens. It is easy to become disillusioned by preparing the same old dinner, in the same old way, at the same old time, in the same old place. There are negative ruts of routine into which we can easily slide. But what if we think on a wider scale? Who made the food we are preparing? By what process did it become available to us? What were the food service workers like? In this way we rise out of the negative associations of the present and broaden our scope of thought. In other words we change our perception. The difference between a monotonous life and an adventuresome life rarely has to do with the places we go or the people we meet. Both life orientations happen right in our home. The answer is in what we perceive our lives to be. Therese of Lisieux lived a life style in Carmel that many would consider monotonous. However, she liked to imagine herself as the infant Jesus' ball. She was happy if he played with it or if he left it in the corner. When we find ourselves in the doldrums, we can look at what we are doing through the eyes of a six year old child, or through the eyes of a Winnie the Pooh bear. What do we see? What would it be like to be God's teddy?

Keeping our eyes on Christ helps us in many ways. It helps us keep the relationships within our family loving and cheerful. Good quality intrafamilial relationships are the best protection against the evils and challenges of the world, as well as for maintaining peace of soul. If praying together is the focal point of the family's existence, it leads to doing what we say we will do without artifice or guile. In so doing we are the same on the outside as we are on the inside. We live what we believe.

How do we cultivate and give witness to the need for prayer in our home? Prayer is the service of the heart and the life of the soul. It gives us immeasurable support in remaining faithful to the every day burdensome aspects of life. True heroism consists in fidelity to the little things that fill our days. Infidelity in little things can be like very large termites eating away at

the foundation of a house. As long as there is no shock
to the house, it stands, but when a shock happens the
house falls. The same is so in family life. If we are not
faithful, a serious temptation can unexpectedly come
to us and we will fall. Therese of Lisieux led an obscure
and uneventful life, yet practiced her little way with
great fidelity. By this way she became a great saint.
She is full of words of wisdom for us:

> Trying to do good to people without God's help
> is no easier than making the sun shine at
> midnight. You discover that you've got to
> abandon all your own preferences, your own
> bright ideas, and guide souls along the road our
> Lord has marked out for them. You mustn't
> coerce them into some path of your own choosing.

Each new day is a time to start over again by clearing
our minds, hearts and souls and refocusing our vision.
We need not litter today with the sawdust of our self-
centered stuff from past days. Life is a journey. Each
day we shake off our sawdust and begin anew.

A community or family is a mix of varied and choice
ingredients amalgamated into unity by the heat of
divine love. Teresa of Avila saw no dichotomy between
seeking the divine and living lovingly with the human.
She tells us: 'I do not believe we could ever attain perfect
love for our neighbor unless it had its roots in the love
of God.' She counseled her sisters: 'All must be friends,
all must be loved, all must be held dear, all must be
helped.' If they find someone difficult to get along with
they should do anything they can for her in a practical
way and also pray for that sister. Teresa of Avila saw
her communities as dovecotes where the sisters live a
life of prayer and are friends with Christ and with each
other. She said: 'Let us strive then always to look at the

virtues and the good qualities which we find in others, and to keep our own grievous sins before our eyes.' She was fond of cleanliness, beauty, order, good taste, courtesy and affection. In a similar vein, and with good and grateful hearts, so should our families strive toward Teresa's community ideals.

> I thank thee, Lord, for this good life,
> For water, oil, wine, wafer, wife,
> For time to do a penance in
> And grace to half forget the sin,
> For father's smile and mother's tears
> And sister's salutary fears,
> For friendships firm and friendships fleeting,
> For adieus and happy meeting,
> For laughter running like a boy,
> For prick of pain foretelling joy,
> For leaps the heart makes at the sense
> On sacramental innocence,
> For having thee to thank and praise,
> Adore and hope for all our days.[2]

Notes

[1]   Text by Michael Gannon ,1955; music by Hendrik Andriessen (1892–1981).
[2]   Francis X. Connolly, 'For Having Thee'.

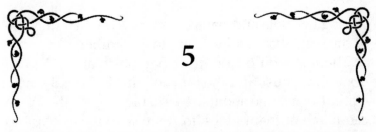

5

THE NEVER ENDING DIRTY DISHES

It can be safe to assume that there are a number of women who are not drawn to the kitchen arts. Meal planning, shopping, food preparation, and clean up leave something to be desired for them. They do not identify with 'kitchen women.' They never liked to cook and do not consider themselves good at it. However, just as lemons can become a lemon meringue pie, meal preparation can become an endeavor of love for their husbands and children. This endeavor of love has a penitential aspect. However, when an innovative woman puts her heart into this penance, she can create a lovely meal. Indeed, love elevates the most menial tasks and makes all things possible.

They seem to be ever present and never ending, these kitchen tasks that are repeated day in and day out. Dirty dishes represent the gaggle of kitchen tasks that can so often be monotonous and tedious. More often than we care to admit, they cause us to groan. Even the mystical homemaker is known to exhale a long sigh, as she thinks 'Will the dirty dishes ever end?' However, underneath the complaint, she knows that 'The Lord dwells among the pots and pans' as Teresa of Avila often reminded her sisters. And the Lord is

among her pots and pans as well, even when they are
in the sink, dirty and waiting to be scrubbed.

There is a bit of fun in boring jobs that need to be
done. One must find the fun, and this is often done by
a mindset change about the task. Blessed are they who
can laugh at themselves, for they shall never cease to
be amused. The more humor we put into a task the
lighter the task becomes. The more love we put in the
work we do, the closer we move toward God. God isn't
looking for deep thoughts or great deeds from us, but
for light-hearted and love-motivated accomplishment
of daily duties. Therese of Lisieux gives us an example
of picking up a pin for the love of God. To pick up a pin
for love is a better mind set than being annoyed by this
small task. An appropriate reaction to the little interrup-
tions that frustrate us is most constructive to our
spiritual growth. John of the Cross said 'Where there is
no love, put love, and you will draw out love.' It seems
we can do the same with humor. Where there is no
humor, put humor, and you will end up laughing. Even
when peeling a potato! John consoles us 'Even though
your obligations and duties are difficult and disagreeable to you, you should not become dismayed, for this
will not always be so... Remember always that everything that happens to you, whether prosperous or
adverse, comes from God so that you neither become
puffed up in prosperity, nor discouraged in adversity.'

Indeed, now and then, in haphazard ways, God's
love, which lies hidden within us, can rise to our
conscious level and overwhelm us with joy. God uses
unexpected and unexciting things to bring us close to
him. With God's love to sustain us, we serve our family
with compassion. 'Let nothing reign in your soul which
does not lead you to sanctity.' With John's words and

with grace, we learn to move easily in difficult, tedious or repetitive situations. Little things done for family members are of great worth in the eyes of Jesus. Tying the shoes of a toddler is just as important as feeding the stranger. Jesus' words: 'What you do for the least of my brothers, that you do unto me' means anyone, including those with whom we live. How dependent little children are upon the adults who care for their needs. How our little acts of care warm the heart of God.

Serenity

There comes a point in life when we may no longer be concerned about telling the difference between good things and bad things. Some things start out looking bad, but the experience can bring us closer to our loved ones and to God than we have ever been. A natural disaster that destroys much of what we own can bring forth great generosity strangers never knew they had. Many stories of goodness can come from a tragedy. Some things start out looking good but wind up terribly. A family celebration can turn into a violent situation. The bad can turn out to be a blessing in disguise. The good can turn out disappointing. This tale illustrates the point: An old man, whom villagers trusted and revered, was often sought out for his wisdom. A farmer came to him and said, 'Wise man, I need your help. A terrible thing has happened. My old horse died and I have no animal to help me plow my field. Is this not the worst thing that could possibly happen?' The old man said 'Maybe so, maybe not.' The farmer got a younger horse and couldn't wait to tell the old man. 'Isn't this the best thing that ever happened?' The wise man said 'Maybe so maybe not.' The lively young horse threw the farmer's son, causing the son to break his leg. 'Isn't this the worst thing that could happen to my son?' the farmer told the man. 'Maybe so, maybe not' the wise man replied. The next day soldiers came and con-scripted every young man but the farmer's son for the army. Motto: We burn up a lot of energy when we think about what is worst or best in our lives. Indeed, we need to live without that type of thinking. By doing so, when things appear to be hopeless we do not lose hope. When life abounds with joy we appreciate it, but are aware that sorrow may be around the corner. That is the rhythm of life. Therese of Lisieux tells us 'When we surrender to discouragement or despair, it is usually because we are thinking too much of the past or the future.' When we ponder deeply we know we have a yearning that nothing on this earth can fully satisfy. We learn to adjust and adapt to the ups and downs of life, and rest in the reality that God is our only lasting source of peace, hope and joy.

As women with a mystic orientation, we know we have to take care of ourselves before we can take care of others. There is always room for improvement in ourselves and in our homes. Many little things can make household tasks safer and easier. When ordinary kitchen duties become significantly irritating for a long period of time, revisions should be made in the kitchen routine department. Low energy is a sign that we need to organize things a little better. We take a good look at what must be done and what is not essential to our well being, both in our homes and in our lives.

In order to conserve energy and simplify work, a time plan helps. We list the days of the week across the top of a page. Next we devise hour by hour segments, from our rising to our going to bed, down the left side of the page. We list what we do during each day in its appropriate time slot and classify what was written down under the categories of work, chore, creative, educational, fitness, recreational, social or spiritual. We know that if the categories are a repetition of work and chore some changes are in order. We pick out the most essential and high energy jobs we have to do, and fit them into our peak energy hours during the day. We try to spread these jobs evenly throughout the week. After each high energy job, we take a period of about ten minutes to rest. We delete nonessential jobs and designate other jobs to our family members. Wives and mothers are not slaves of the house, they are teachers. Home maintenance is a family affair and age appropriate jobs should be taught and assigned to each person in the house. When the subject of chores comes up, there can be conflict and opposition among family members. However, more importantly the members can balance and complement each other, which can be used well in work distribution and in keeping the house tidy. When we include family members in a difficult task, it reduces the effort and energy needed to complete the task.

When we evaluate our daily routine, we look at how we work at a task. Why is this job necessary? When is the best time to do it? Who would be the best person to do it? What is the best way to do it?

Easy Does it

Housekeeping is an unending and sometimes overwhelming job. Instead of cleaning the whole house in one day, we can do a little cleaning each day. We vacuum the floors one day, dust the next, clean the sinks, tub and shower the following day, or we can clean one room a day. We can do light once overs which will avoid accumulation of dirt. We can alternate standing and walking jobs with sitting jobs, heavy tasks with light tasks, and jobs that are done with others with jobs that can be done alone. Here are some other helpful hints for energy conservation: Before beginning a task, gather all items needed to complete the task. Set up work areas to permit a coordinated flow of activities during the task. Place items in the order of use and within easy reach. Take short rest breaks during a heavy or tedious task. Rest before becoming exhausted. Work at a slow, steady pace. Sit to work when possible. Chair type and table height should facilitate proper posture. Place one foot on a block or step to rest your back. Use both hands in opposite and smooth flowing motions when possible. Use strong muscle groups and large joints to do the work. Use stabilizers such as suction bases, vises, stabilized lid openers, clamps, or non skid mats to avoid holding objects in hands for long periods of time. Avoid haste, worry and anxiety. Use light-weight utensils, containers, dishes, pans, bowls etc. Cook large quantities of food and freeze individual servings. Use casserole dishes for cooking and serving. Soak dirty utensils and pans immediately after use. Use narrow shelves, lazy susans, gliding pull out shelves and peg boards for easy access. Avoid compulsive buying and live simply.

Organizing family time and activities is helped by a centrally-located bulletin board. Not only is this a place for a large calendar, but also a place for shopping lists, household telephone numbers, a notepad for jotting down reminders and an inspirational thought, prayer or picture. A kitchen should be set up to promote safety and ease while working in it. More accidents occur in the home than anywhere else. The sad thing is that most of these accidents could be prevented with careful planning and correct use of equipment and appliances. In this age of accumulation of stuff, where kitchen gadgets abound, it can be a dangerous place in which to work.

Several simple precautions can help avoid accidents or injury. Always use padded potholders when moving a hot container. Whenever possible, slide heavy objects instead of lifting them. Select kitchen tools that have non heat conducting handles. Ladle hot liquids to prevent spills. Remove other hot foods with a strainer basket or slotted spoon instead of lifting the pot to drain or pour. Select knives and other utensils with large handles so that they can be grasped more easily. Check the temperature of the hot water coming through the faucets so that it does not scald. Use a wheeled table or cart to move things to the table. Wear suitable and safe clothing while working in the kitchen because long loose sleeves and frills are hazardous. Eliminate protuberances you could bump into or small rugs you could slip on. It is good to have a flat edged rubber mat on the floor by your sink to help prevent slipping on water splashes. Carpets and rugs should be well secured with no frayed or curled edges. Furniture and handrails are sturdy and wobble free. Clutter on kitchen counters and other work surfaces is kept at a minimum. Rubber or plastic sink mats help prevent breaking dishes or glasses. Knives and other sharp or pointed objects are in a safe place. Overhead cupboards are kept closed and electrical sockets not overloaded with appliances. Smoke detectors and fire extinguishers are installed at appropriate places and checked regularly.

Plan a specific place for everything, storing utensils used at the same time in one place. Cut down on unnecessary items, the ones that are frustrating, dangerous or only used occasionally. When removing light objects from a high shelf use a step stool and place one foot on a higher step to ease low back strain. Use the assistance of gravity whenever possible. Carry heavy objects as close to the body as possible. Avoid carrying unbalanced loads, a heavy object in one hand and nothing in the other hand. Take advantage of objects with casters, (buckets, cases etc). A slightly raised counter edge will help prevent items from rolling and falling onto the floor. Sliding rather than swinging doors on cabinets prevents head on collisions. Pull out shelves and drawers, or lazy susans reduce reaching into the back of cabinets.

Our kitchen makes a statement about ourselves: what we value, our interests, our lifestyle and our beliefs. The kitchen is a meeting place for sharing a wide variety of topics. Examples range from perplexing struggles to spiritual insights to the ordinary communications of life. Family is our greatest asset in daily household management. Full participation in household management will help each member to enjoy more leisure and recreational activities. It is not so much our limitations that necessitate our help in routine activities, but rather the fair way, the happy way, and the sharing way that comes when a family pulls together. If we teach our children to enjoy food preparation activities we will find delighted little chefs at our elbows. Work is simpler when each family member is responsible for a part of each meal: buying food, preparing it, setting the table or cleaning up. We can encourage children's culinary arts with a cookbook geared to their age levels. Harness their energies and develop responsibility by teaching them good habits and a pattern for later life. Children can clear the table, clean up, carry in groceries, or take out the trash. Teenagers can assist with, or do, light shopping.

We Gather Together

Meals can be plain, simply prepared, moderate in proportion and nourishing. When we regularly share family meals we get to know others at the table better. It is true that the beauty of dining together as a family has decreased in importance. This is unfortunate and needs to be corrected. Meals eaten while standing by the microwave or on the run, or eaten quickly while doing other things do not give us a rest stop in the day. We miss so much by continued use of take outs, drive-throughs and food machines. We miss so much when we eat in a rush… including really tasting what we eat.

The kitchen, from which many lessons can be learned, is the main area for caring and sharing, (or for fights) in a family. It is the heartbeat of the home. Dining together as a family is more important than attending the children's sports events or taking them to various lessons. A very simple meal can be a time of intersection, of coming together and relaxing from the cares of the day. Eating is the most basic and the most fundamental activity of our lives because it maintains life in our bodies, and can be a time of joy, reunion and communion. Loud dissonant music during meals has an unfavorable effect on our communication and our digestive abilities. Do we listen to the TV news while we eat? Combining meals with hot button issues, problem solving and other items that cause tension prevents the renewal that shared meals can bring. It is best to leave these things for another time. The family meal time is not the place for mean spirited arguing, picking on each other, bickering, nagging or other degrading exchanges. Easy conversation and encouraging words enhance table banter.

Elise Boulding wrote in *Children and Solitude*:

> In homes where silence is lived, the child finds it easy and comfortable to turn to it. In a large and noisy family (like my own) the period of hush that begins every meal sweeps like a healing wind over all the cross currents that have built up in the previous hours and leaves the household clean and sweet.

Jesus is the unseen person at our family meals. Awareness of his presence maintains peace and unity by mutual respect and quality conversation. What would Jesus say to each family member seated at the table? What would each family member say to him? What can we do to make our meal conversations and table manners better? How can we be a positive influence on those around us? Jesus tells us that our light should not be kept under a bushel basket. Our light is meant to shine forth. We cannot let the best that is in us stay inside us. That would be unfair for everyone around us. When we let our light shine we unconsciously give others the okay to let their lights shine. The lights that begin to shine inside our home at the family dinner table, bring a beautiful light to the entire neighborhood.

Because eating is a necessity of life, it is good to look at how and when we eat. Does our kitchen resemble a fast food eatery or a filling station? If we eat because of negative reasons we need to acknowledge and define those reasons and work with them in appropriate ways. What and why we eat can reveal how we feel about ourselves. Do we open the refrigerator when we are bored, lonely, depressed, anxious or stressed? Does eating help us feel loved, accepted or secure? Eating can become an addiction. It should not be a response to fear, emotional extremes, discomfort, or a way to avoid problems. We may gravitate toward our comfort foods when life becomes difficult. We can also cook or bake as a response to an inability to cope with an issue and then eat what we prepared. We should periodically look at the various reasons why we eat. It is so easy to automatically eat a particular comfort food, one after the other, until it is gone. What are the reasons why we do this? What are the behaviors, social customs and cultural influences that affect our poor eating habits? We eat to live, and when we are influenced by the right motivation, eating is a joyous occasion. If we keep in mind that our bodies are the housing of our souls, and a great gift from God to us, we will be more attentive to our responsibility to God and to each other to take care of these gifts.

Keeping a home clean and in order is a way to pursue holiness in the ordinary activities of life. Here are some guidelines for the mystic home: If you open it, close it. If you drop it, pick it up. If you spill it, wipe it up. If you empty it, fill it. If you move it, put it back. If you break it, fix it. If you use it up, put it on the shopping list.

Mystics are not yet saints and when household tasks and familial problems seem to overwhelm us, we react to our home situation with dark thoughts. Who hasn't thought or heard: 'All I am around here is a cook and a maid. Nobody listens to what I have to say. I work myself to a frazzle, and no one appreciates me' etc. We break a dish, burn the casserole in the oven or realize the soup has boiled over on the stove. Everything seems to be in a mess, yet the pursuit of holiness keeps us in the right frame of mind. Dealing with the quirks, weaknesses and differences in our family members, and in ourselves, in an appropriate manner is a way of becoming holy. We know that God is working in our personal messes and in our family situations. We are nurtured in this growth in love in known and unknown ways. Our devotion to our family, or religious community, creates deep love and unity. Love is not based on how we feel at the moment. A woman cannot create a family home unless she loves the members of her family beyond measure. A sister cannot create a convent home unless she loves her sisters beyond measure. Most work in these living situations is necessary and ordinary. Toilets need cleaning, clothes need washing, grass needs mowing. Routine tasks can become as boring inside a cloister as they can inside a home.

What is important is not what we get or don't get out of what we do because that always changes. It is what we give. We do what we do with great love, and by doing a task in this way we contribute to the good of the family or the community. Through day in and day out devotion to duty, the truths of God are woven into the material of the day. This helps time bound fragmentations dissolve into the eternal timelessness and truths of God. Grace and the truths of God help parents talk and act in such a way that their children know they are loved and valued. Grace and God's truths help husband and wife face relational issues and problems instead of losing themselves in excess work, shopping, eating or other addictive behaviors. They also assist parents in focusing more on solutions to problems, than on the problems themselves. Grace and God's truths also keep parents on the straight and narrow road to God and work in mysterious, beautiful and unexpected ways.

God's Best

There is nothing like a mother. The full realization of this phrase is felt by the heart after she has died. Her life of love and service is so very precious in the heart of God. He loves mothers very much, that is why he made so many of them! That is why he gave one of them the greatest honor the world has known. Mary teaches mothers many things, the first of which is how to pray. Prayer is the mainstay of the day. Where would mothers be without prayer? Quite lost. Prayer keeps a mother grounded and focused when she is preoccupied with the needs of her little ones: cooking, clothing, sheltering, teaching, guiding, nursing, consoling, forgiving, warning, comforting, all happen in an often unrecognized and endless round. Dostojewski sees the heroism in the routine of daily duties: 'To be a hero for a moment, for an hour, is easier than to bear the heroism of everyday life. Accept life as it is—gray and monotonous, that activity for which no one praises you, that heroism which no one notes, which draws no attention to yourself. He (she) who bears the colorless challenge of life and still remains a man (woman) is indeed a hero!'

Therese of Lisieux gives mothers some comforting thoughts: 'Love can accomplish all things, Things that are most impossible become easy where love is at work … Remember that nothing is small in the eyes of God. Do all that you do with love.' She reflects from her own

life 'I must anticipate the desires of others... show that
we are much obliged, very honored to be able to render
service. The good Lord wants me to forget myself in
order to give pleasure to others.' Forgetting oneself is
so common for mothers. More often than not mothers
put the needs of their children first and go without.

Edith Stein, a brilliant woman, helps women along
their road with these words:

> When we wake up in the morning, the troubles
> and duties of the day crowd around us. When
> will we do this? When that? One wants to jump
> up in a rush and dash away. You had better take
> the reins in your hand and say: Whoa! None of
> this must come near me just yet... It is impor-
> tant to have a quiet corner where one can
> commune with God as if nothing else existed,
> and it is important to do this on a daily basis.
> The obvious time appears to me to be the
> morning hours before the daily work begins.[1]

When a woman gets up in the morning and gives that
time to God in prayer, while her family sleeps, she can
experience great peace. It also becomes very important
because she knows that at times prayer is the only
thing that holds when everything else fails. Edith
continues:

> One finds time for so many useless things: to
> read up on all sorts of useless stuff in books,
> magazines and newspapers, to sit around in
> cafes and gab away a quarter hour, a half hour.
> Shouldn't it be possible then to eke out a
> morning hour during which one does not
> scatter oneself but concentrates, to gain strength
> in order to cope with the entire day?[2]

Trusting in God, Edith tells us that it is important to find out what works best and then to make good use of it. She goes on in a poetic vein:

> Be therefore steadfast, calm and true,
> your God is at your side.
> Through storm and night he'll see you through,
> with conscience as your guide.[3]

Reports from people who were near Edith during her week of imprisonment at Auschwitz say she was a woman of remarkable interior strength who gave courage to her fellow prisoners. She helped mothers feed and bathe their little children, even when the mothers had given up hope and were neglecting these tasks. One woman who survived the war wrote a description of Edith during the time their group was waiting to be transported to the East:

> She was not afraid, but I cannot express it better except by saying that she seemed to carry such a heavy burden of suffering that even when she did smile every once and a while, it made one even sadder... She had the thought of impending suffering; not her own, for she had long accepted it, but the suffering that was awaiting the others. Her whole appearance, as I see her in my mind's eye sitting in the barrack, still reminds me of a Pietà without Christ.[4]

It is known that women in these concentration camps shared recipes with each other. It helped them reflect on pleasant childhood memories, reaffirmed their identity and helped them bear the burden of their imprisonment.

The spiritual road is not an easy one on which to tread. It is not for those with feeble hearts or weak souls. At times we may wonder who we are or where we are going. When we are perplexed, upset, frightened or fearful we ponder Teresa of Avila's often quoted words:

> Let nothing disturb you.
> Let nothing frighten you.
> For all things pass save God
> Who does not change.
> Be patient and at the last
> You will find All fulfillment.
> Hold God and nothing
> Will fail you.
> For he alone is all.[5]

Notes

[1]   Edith Stein, *Die Frau. Ihre Aufgabe nach Natur und Gnade* (Louvain und Freiburg, E. Nauwelaerts und Herder, 1959), volume V, pp. 88–90.

[2]   Edith Stein, 'Who can sleep on the night that God became man?'

[3]   Edith Stein, 'Am Steuer' ('At the Helm').

[4]   Lucie Bromberg-Rosenthal as quoted in P. Hamans, *Edith Stein and Companions. On the Way to Auschwitz* (San Francisco, CA: Ignatius Press, 2010), pp. 85–86.

[5]   This brief poem is known as her 'Bookmark; it was found in her prayer book after her death in 1582.

6

LET'S GO ON A PICNIC

 picnic invites us to lay our troubles aside and spend some time just having fun. Picnics can happen on the spur of the moment or they can be well planned. Their locations are vast: the backyard, park, living room, woods, seashore hillside or lakeside. No matter where the site, a picnic is an opportunity for eating, playing games, singing, sharing, relaxing, reconnecting and reminiscing. These activities can be for a family of two, a multi-generation family reunion, a parish, team, company or school. Why, it has even been said that teddy bears and little critters of the forest have picnics. Of course a most important thing in these gatherings is the food. Ah, glorious food! It can range from finger tidbits to full fledged gourmet meals.

Picnics bring many happy memories to mind. There can be picnics for no reason, picnics to celebrate God's blessings or picnics to celebrate different holidays or family occasions. Irish Soda Bread is a favorite of many and is made, not only to celebrate St Patrick's Day, but on any occasion that is special. Before putting the dough in the oven, the baker cuts a big cross on the top of the dough with a knife. As the bread rises in the oven, the loaf slowly browns and makes the cross more defined. Watching the bread rise and sniffing the aroma that fills the kitchen is a real treat. Almost any kind of food can be used for picnic fare, even the leftovers in the refrigerator. Food usually represents something of who we are, where we came from and what we care about. We could have a picnic and ask each person to bring their favorite food. Teresa of Avila would bring her figs, John of the Cross would bring his asparagus and Therese of Lisieux would bring the best of all, eclairs!

Picnics remind us that we need to take time out for leisure in each day and to use Sunday as a day of rest if possible. Leisure is our time out from work and cares. On Sunday we can avoid unnecessary work and make the day special by enjoying a treat, like a coffee cake, with the family. We can eat together at a leisurely pace, and light a special candle. We can even sing special songs or say special prayers. Sunday is a time to break our normal daily routine by reading a new or favorite book, drinking a special tea or doing other things we do not do during the week: paint a picture, listen to classical music, visit a new place, write a letter, poem or play or have a talent show or song fest. Sunday is a special day to refresh our spirit and renew our life with God.

On a picnic we can see how things connect us with God's creative gifts. We eat bread which grows from wheat, out of the earth through the warmth of the sun which also gives us heat and light. Rain waters the plants, quenches our thirst, and washes and refreshes us. We feel awesome when we experience the manifestations of sun and rain on the wheat fields or in a rainbow. Other growing flora and fauna capture us and ravish us with their beauty. Wildflowers, plants, rivers, streams, woods and cloud formations take us out of ourselves and give us a new, refreshing perspective.

If we planned a picnic what interesting person would we invite to it? John of the Cross tells us: 'The soul of one who loves God always swims in joy, always keeps holiday, and it is always in a mood for singing.' That sounds like a sentence for a good time. If we asked John of the Cross to come along, he would most likely take us on a nature walk. One of his favorite recreational activities was to go outside and discover spiritual delights in everyday surroundings. We can imagine him sitting under a tree and writing 'Scattering a thousand graces, He passed through these groves in haste, and left them by his glance alone, clothed in beauty.' John often took his confreres out for a hike and spent days on the hillsides. They basked in the beauties of the flowers and the fields. Nature fueled John's burning love for God, which is so vividly illustrated in his poetry. It is said that nature was John's primary interest in the physical realm. Natural landscapes spoke to him of the majesty of God. Be it flowers by day or stars by night, he was in awe of the bounties of God's creative powers. One could find John in his room, with his elbows on the windowsill, gazing out at nature's wonders. He wrote in his *Spiritual Canticle*: 'My beloved is the mountains, and lonely wooded valleys, strange islands, and resounding rivers, the whistling of love stirring breezes, the tranquil night at the time of the rising dawn, silent music, sounding solitude, the supper that refreshes and deepens love.'

One day a sister asked John why, when she went near the pond in the garden, the frogs on the surface jumped into the water and hid themselves in the depths of the pond. The frogs did this almost before they heard the sound of her footsteps. John answered that the frogs felt safe in the depths of the pond and that this is what she must likewise do: flee from sin and hide herself in God.

Another time John asked a nun about her way of prayer. She said that she looked upon God's beauty and rejoiced that he possessed it. So impressed was John by her reply that for several days he spoke about many wonderful things concerning the beauty of God. John was so taken by the wonders of God's beauty here on earth that he wrote about them in five stanzas of his *Spiritual Canticle*, which has remained a spiritual classic to this day.

It is said that John is the greatest poet in the Spanish language. Yet, such greatness came from humble beginnings. John was born in Spain, in the small dusty town of Fontiveros in 1542. His father, Gonzalo, met his mother, Catalina, when he made a business trip to Medina del Campo. Catalina was a poor, humble weaver while Gonzalo came from a noble and wealthy family. Gonzalo experienced bitter opposition from his family about Catalina, but in spite of that, he followed his heart and married her. His family disowned him because of his marriage.

John was the youngest of three sons. The oldest, Francisco, was twelve years older than John, and a dear treasure throughout his life. The middle son died while still a child, seemingly of malnutrition. John never knew his father. Gonzalo died of a painful illness shortly after John was born. Catalina told John about his father through loving reminiscences. After her husband's death, she was left destitute. Her husband's relatives refused to help her. She had very little support, except for her faith in God. As a single parent, she struggled and raised her two sons despite deprivation and rejection. John's youth was warm with his mother's love and strong in faith. His early schooling took place at an institution that cared for poor children. After working and studying at a Jesuit college, at the age of twenty-one John entered the Carmelites in Medina del Campo. He was ordained a priest in 1567. Later in that year he met Teresa of Avila and joined her in establishing a new family within the Carmelite Order. The remaining years of his life were a time of hard work and many trials. After much suffering John died in Ubeda in 1591. He is known as one of the greatest contemplatives and teachers of mystical theology. One can sum up his life with his words 'And I saw the river over which every soul must pass to reach the kingdom of heaven and the name of that river was suffering—and I saw the boat which carries souls across the river and the name of that boat was love.'

When we are at a restful place in the still woods, John gently explains to us why a deep life, with God at its center, is so important. This orientation gives us the grace to love God more and know ourselves better. When we focus on God we are not held slaves by materialism, projects, social expectations, cultural norms or any other pesky appetite that keeps us alienated from our true selves. Social realities can easily pull us away from God's love. We can become so fragmented by endless preoccupations and looking to popular persons or trends for our identity or affirmation. When our identity is fixed on Jesus we are not swayed by what society tells us because we know who resides in the center of our hearts. God's living flame burns within us, and keeps us on that mysterious dark trail that ultimately leads to God.

When we are on a hike in the woods, we rest somewhere in a quiet place and are awestruck by silence.
What whets the appetite for spiritual nourishment? It
is silence. When we realize the importance of silence,
we make a time for it in our daily lives. Silence is
essential for the mystic sojourn. To know the beauty of
silence is rare, and to find time for it is a challenge. We
are so engrossed by discoveries in communication and
technology, we are led to believe that silence is only a
void to be filled or a clumsy gap in communication. If
we experience how silence gives life, we know how a
multitude of words can dissipate and deplete us in
known and unknown ways. Silence restores us to our
authentic selves, especially after we experience an out
pouring of our own words or hear non stop talk from
others. The first screw that loosens in a person's head
is often the one that holds the tongue in place. Abraham
Lincoln said: 'Better to remain silent and be thought a
fool than to speak and remove all doubt.' For people
who are accustomed to talking a lot, tongue control can
be a struggle. John of the Cross offers some advice.
'Great wisdom is to be able to keep silence and to look
neither at the words nor at the deeds, nor at the lives of
others.' He also says: 'Better to conquer the tongue than
to fast on bread and water.' Silence is augmented by
limiting superficial talk, and turning down the volume
controls. Many things are born in silence, such as deep
prayer and creative ideas. The mysterious presence of
God is at the center of the soul and the language of the
soul is receptive silence.

What is really important is not what we say or do.
It is our ability to increase, by ever so little, the amount
of quiet love that exists in the world through our
various activities. Husbands and wives in a good

marriage, or good spiritual friends find value, comfort and a homey peace when they are together in silence. The need to fill unexpected silence with words is not necessary. When visiting a person who is sick, silence can nurture courtesy, respect and healing. Silence places the need to chatter in the background. The silence of God's love is too great for any expression. The book of Wisdom tells us: 'When night was at its deepest point and all was stilled and silent, your Word O Lord came down.' To this Word we listen, listen, and listen again.

We need more silence in our lives. We need to recognize the gold in silence. Silence and stillness create a sense of wonder, a sense of mystery, an experience of the sacred in everything. Beauty has a reality beyond our comprehension or perceptions which teaches us things we cannot put into words or categories. Silence and stillness help us discover our infinite worth as seen through the eyes of God our Father, even though we never truly comprehend this. We are stretched and deepened because we do not understand and cannot really describe God. We open up to greater beauty, truth and goodness, and are more alert and receptive to our inner voice. Silence and solitude broaden our contemplative dimension. By avoiding complacency and mediocrity, we awaken to the wisdom and wonder of each moment. Silence and solitude balance our busy lives by refreshing our bodies and minds and renewing our spirits and souls. We know that the joy we have will be tempered with sorrow; we are more aware of the holiness and hardships in life. We are stilled and expanded. We are comfortable with silence and solitude no matter what they bring us. We celebrate life with exuberance yet instinctively turn to the sacred still point within ourselves where we ponder our potential as children of God.

When we are at that still point, it reveals many things to us. Similar to being in a quiet forest, be it actual or a pictorial refuge in the mind, it is a place where our thoughts are clear and sharp. No long thoughts are needed to know how easy it is to fall into the sink holes of sin. Catherine of Siena, a young, Italian, Dominican lay woman and doctor of the Church, called sin a deadly vomit. What are some of the reasons why notorious sinners live in this vomit? An enormous ego says there is no God but me. A God outside the self does not exist. There is no concept about the deadly poisons of sin. Sinful acts are used to make money, to exploit, to dehumanize, to get pleasure or do anything else that causes harm. The denial of sin is epidemic. Possessions, health, beauty, youth and other self-enhancers are addictions that enslave the heart and take the place of God. Excessive and inordinate behavior and activities that obscure or obliterate God's love in the world take on a life of their own and never offer complete or lasting satisfaction. The sinner never gets enough. He or she is forever chasing pleasure and other pursuits and is seldom content.

Mystics know how false gods can imprison sinners. To be centered on Christ is to maintain a stable peace in the soul. Awareness of the many danger zones on the spiritual path keeps one's attention focused on where one's feet are going. It is true that everyone sins. However the grace of God is our temptation detector and it flashes a warning when we come to forbidden territory. We know when to stop when we are too much into the entertainments and allurements of the world. Life is full of temptations, but we will not be overcome by them. Every sin, no matter how small, hurts God, others, and most of all ourselves. Sin weakens and sickens the human family. When we are tempted, we switch our mind set to the love of Jesus and gaze at Christ crucified. The cross gives us courage. Staying away from that which tempts us makes progress on the spiritual path easier and faster. We keep looking at the top of the mountain, the summit of the spiritual life, where our wills will always be united to the will of God.

Mystics pray for sinners to crack a little bit so that God's love can shine in them. Mothers often say extra prayers and make extra sacrifices for their wayward children who have strayed from the path of God's love. A shining example of this is Monica, who prayed for her son Augustine for thirty years, therefore becoming a model of patience and perseverance for all times. After leading a life of deep sin, Augustine converted and became a great bishop and an influential doctor of the Church. Where sin abounds, grace can abound more. God works in mysterious ways, especially within the darkness of a sinner. A little self-knowledge can go a long way. Self-knowledge defeats self-centeredness and opens the crack wider. Prayer is the key that opens the heart held captive by false gods. When we pray we want to pray more. The more we practice virtue, doing that which pleases God, the easier virtue becomes. If we clothe ourselves with Christ's love each morning, the decisions of each day should reflect that love. Choices are always present in our duties and responsibilities and these choices require the most love we have to give. No choice is insignificant. We try to respond the best we can to what we think God is asking of us. Through perseverance, trust and patience, we remain stable in our determination to live the teachings of Christ. When people or situations in our Church annoy or upset us, we look to Christ. We remember God takes care of his Church, which is more than a mere institution. It is the bride of Christ.

As we sit in the woods surrounded by silence we reflect upon the words of John Henry Newman: 'May he support us all the day long, till the shades lengthen, and the evening comes, and the busy world is hushed, and the fever of life is over, and our work is done. Then in his mercy may he give us a safe lodging and a holy rest and peace at the last.'[1]

Home is Where the Heart is

A woman's home is her castle and her family is her greatest treasure. The home is a place where love has boundless expressions, from adding on a room to taking out the garbage. Love is measured by the way family members treat each other, especially during times of tension. A good thing we can do with free time is spend it with our family. With a look under the surface of situations, we can find jocularities in the difficulties of life, amusement in the jobs we dislike and serenity when our world outside is frenzied and confused. Often we find the miraculous in the ridiculous. An uncluttered home is a reminder to keep our lives uncluttered. The blessings in our home remind us to frequently count our personal blessings. If we enjoy the serendipity that comes from doing something in a new way we diminish our chances of getting into a rut. It is good to learn from the simplicity and directness of children: Share everything. Play fair. Don't hurt people or animals. Don't say mean things. Say you're sorry when you hurt someone. Learn a little, think a little, work, rest, play and pray every day. Use the magic words: please and thank you. Stick together. Help each other. Don't go with strangers. See the wonder in little things.

We also learn much from the elder members of our family. They have a lot to teach us. Who among us has not sat at the feet of a dear old grandmother and heard her wise stories? Her narratives of wit and wisdom are to be savored and remembered.

We have all seen children and adults entranced by different little insects moving about. Teresa of Avila uses young silkworms to show us how we are to let God work in us. Young silkworms nourish themselves by eating mulberry leaves. When they reach a certain stage they attach themselves to the twigs of the mulberry bush and spin cocoons around themselves. Unseen inside the cocoon the silkworm transforms into a beautiful butterfly. God is the only one who sees this change. We make ourselves available to God so that he may reside and freely work in our hearts. With the help of grace, we get rid of parts of ourselves that take away from his love and add elements that enhance his love. When we break from the cocoon of self, our transformation in Christ is greater than the external change of the butterfly. We emerge from the darkness of sin and reflect Christ's light to all.

That Frequent Shadow

It seems we all do it. Some of us do it every few hours, others every day. What is this common element to which we are bound? It is worry. Someone said worry is like rust upon a blade, and so it is. The rust mars the gleam and dulls the sharpness of the blade. Worry gives imagined or small things big shadows. It is the dark-room in which negatives can develop. To help us stay in the sunlight, we can dwell on this phrase: Never trouble trouble, 'til trouble troubles you. It is only human to worry now and then. A key that unlocks the door to a contemplative demeanor is a reduction of worry. Here is a little story to help with this concern: A CEO drove into her driveway at the end of a long hard day. She had many concerns and troubles with which to contend. A flat tire made her late for work. Her secretary quit. Co-workers were bringing their troubles to her all afternoon. And now her car had an annoying sound in the engine. As she walked toward the back door of her home, she paused briefly at a small tree. She touched the tips of the branches with both hands. After opening the back door she underwent an amazing transformation. She had a smile on her face. She embraced her husband and kindly greeted her three small children. What happened? What was that myste-rious action with the tree? The CEO would tell you that the tree was her worry tree. She knew she could not help having troubles on the job that cause worry. What mattered was that troubles and their consequent worry did not belong in her house with her husband and children. So she just hung them on the tree every night when she came home. Then in the morning she picked them up. However, the funny thing was that when she came out in the morning to pick them up, there were not as many as she remembered hanging up on the tree the night before.

Outdoors, on a balmy Autumn afternoon, we can awaken to the sacredness of life. Who hasn't lain down on her back in the grass, felt the sun on her face, heard the songs of the birds, insects and rustle of the trees, and smelled the fragrance of earth, plants and flowers? As we look up into the sky we might notice wild geese migrating, flying in a V formation in the October sky. It seems that they fly seventy percent further when they fly in this formation, in each others slip stream. The strong ones go in front and the weak ones fly behind them and they are routinely changing places. There is a mutual affirmation in the honking that goes with the flying. Teresa of Avila was a great one for formation in community. Community members develop virtues, ordinary good manners, courtesy, graciousness, gentleness, encouragement and periodic changes in leadership. How well the geese give us an example of this. An environment in which everyone is valued and everybody matters is conducive to growth in community and in family life.

Teresa of Avila was a great one for laughter and seeing the lighter side of things. If we cannot laugh at ourselves we are missing a good joke. We may giggle as we look at the Autumn sky and imagine ourselves as a twinkling star or a floating cloud. Happiness comes from within. If we are not happy within ourselves we will not be happy with others. Our words reflect our degree of happiness. A bit of a poem puts it this way: Keep watch on your words, my loved ones, for words are wonderful things. They are sweet like the bee's fresh honey, but like the bees they have terrible stings. How often have positive and joyful words neutralized a tense situation? A cheerful remark can brighten up a gloomy environment like a sunbeam piercing through dark clouds.

Our Therese of Lisieux gives us a very good lesson here. She wrote it three months before she died. In loving others she knew she was loving Jesus and was able to do this only because Jesus was living in her heart. 'You know very well that never would I be able to love my sisters as you love them, unless you O my Jesus, loved them in me.' That is a sentence worth a hundred meditations. Again Therese said 'It is not what you do that matters, but the love with which you do it.' Our love of God must be channeled to our love for our family, and others close to us. Christ loves in us. The heart of a mystic is characterized by an ability to be compassionate and gentle in most situations. This is because the heart is animated by love.

In Praise of Play

Volleyball is enjoyed by all, including those behind the cloister wall. Carmelite nuns usually have two periods each day for recreation. This is their play time. A story is told about a novice who wanted to pray during recreation time. Teresa set her straight. She told the novice that she could pray if she liked but Teresa said she would rather be with the Lord at recreation with her sisters. It is a good idea to have a recreation time for the family. They could play board games, do handcrafts or other hobbies together. As in the nun's daily schedule, it would serve as a rest from the fast pace of the day. So often family members lead very busy lives with time taken up with things to do, places to go or people to see. Bodies become weary, minds tired and spirits worn in the rush and whirl of the day.

A daily, or weekly, family recreation, would re create balance and priority. What is more important: Rushing around to different entertainments alone away from home, or doing a restful activity together inside the home?

Play is a time for fun that can permeate every corner of our lives. We all know someone with a playful nature. Such a nature cannot be analyzed. Play is not planned; there are no goals, no effort and no schedules. It has its own time and space, and happens when we are immersed in what we are doing. We lose our sense of time, awareness of our external environment and conscious sense of ourselves. Watch young girls playing hopscotch or jumping rope. They are completely absorbed in the game, happy watching who is hopping or jumping and unaware of what is happening beyond the borders of the game. Time stands still for them. It is a time apart from real time for the duration of the game.

The sight of a butterfly fluttering around a flower, the sound of a bird's song, the aroma of a pine forest, the taste of an ice cream cone, the feel of a soft teddy bear brightens up the day with a lighthearted sensory refreshment. Play can inspire and develop creativity; a fort designed and built in the back yard, a poem written with a jocular flair, a song composed, unique in melody and nonsensical in lyric. We need play because it rejuvenates, relaxes and uplifts us by a carefree focus. A whimsical remark fragments tension at a serious meeting. We find an element of amusement in an insignificant task which lightens routine. A change of attitude turns mundane work into a bit of play. A sense of reverence makes the commonplace beautiful. A hectic day becomes calm by leisurely contemplative moments. When we find moments of relaxation in our work day, we look at discouraging moments with a light heart.

Play is rarely found in expensive purchases, ego wants, programmed activities or elaborate vacations. In play we grasp what is here and now and turn it into a joyful experience. Play captivates us by giving us the freedom to focus on what is most fascinating at this particular time. We find magic and mystery in the delicate designs on a spider's web or a seashell, or in the beauty of the color and shape of a flower. We find unanticipated knowledge through simple attentiveness, surprise from the treasures in serendipity and sudden intuitions in the reality of the present moment. Children are naturals at living in the present moment. It completely holds their focus with an openness and sense of wonder. As adults we easily lose these qualities, but they can be regained. At play, self-defeating defenses vanish because we give up control. We let go and let be. We need not worry about security or success since true play experiences all creation as a gift to be shared. We are receptive to these gifts with a trust in the giver and an openness to the given. There is no desire to take or keep these gifts. Rather, there is a childlike trust that graciously receives all gifts, by simply allowing things to unfold and believing that all will be well. We let things happen rather than make things happen. We are aware that there is action in non action and accept things as they are rather than make attempts to change things according to our wants. We drink the refreshment we find in the unpressured time we share with family, and note there is great beauty in simplicity: the charm of a sleeping baby, children engrossed in quiet fantasy amusements, the quiet enjoyment shared by husband and wife during a leisurely walk in the evening's twilight. As we take time to enjoy the simple pleasures of life, we learn to coast through unexpected free periods of time with the delight of a child. Play is renewing, and reconnects communication in families in the midst of carefree activity buoyed with a genial good humor.

Play times can be opportunities to better connect with family members in greater clarity and depth. Now and then we can meet and share our responses to a few of these statements: My favorite toy. My most influential toy. My first memories. My favorite nursery rhymes, bedtime stories and lullabies. Secret or magic places in my family home, backyard, neighborhood and hometown. My cherished childhood memories. My first train, plane and boat ride. My favorite songs and super stars. My longest journey. The wonders in my world. The lessons (dance, music, etc.) in my life. My heroes and heroines. The accomplishments of which I am most proud. That which is special about my childhood and adolescence. My friends and foes. My hopes, dreams failures, successes. Persons who have had a special influence in my life. Other influences in my life (art, theatre, literature, etc.). My likes and dislikes. Funny things that have happened to me. Heartaches and trials. Joys and exaltations. Reflections on our responses help us to rediscover ourselves.

Rebecca is a working mother with two young school age children. As a child she did not need things that were plugged in or that required batteries to give her joy. She had the opportunity to ride a bike and felt the wind blow against her face which was a glorious experience. She had a doll and gave it tender loving care, which in turn gave her moments of peace and contentment. Of course there was, and still is, 'L. J.' her tattered teddy, who comforts her in sorrow and shares in her joy. He is always there, day and night, to listen or hug and never tells her secrets to anyone. Yet her greatest of all pleasures came from sand. When she built a castle with sand she found it to be the grandest of all things to do. That was a great delight for her, knowing she provided a home for a beautiful princess. The walls protected this princess from the crashing ocean waves. Rebecca dug a trench that surrounded the entire castle and marveled at the water swirling in her moat. Inevitably the sea spilled into the gateway and washed away the castle, but great joy was always there because Rebecca knew she could rebuild it again.

Wonder is enhanced by a sense of awe, humor, and great appreciation for the miracles in, and the amusing aspects of life. It is an important part of the grandeur of creation and the beauty of love. We wonder at a commonplace thing and find it magical and mystical because God's graces shine through it like a rainbow. Wonder gives us an inner freedom that delights in the present. Wonder is necessary for us to understand the gift of ourselves and the wondrous love of God. Similar to a celestial hymn, wonder harmonizes with reverence and respect, and has an enchanting melody that lifts us into the mystic realm of God.

For the beauty of the earth,
For the beauty of the skies,
For the love who from our birth
Over and around us lies,
Lord of all to thee we raise
This our hymn of grateful praise.

For the beauty of each hour
Of the day and of the night,
Hill and vale, and tree and flower,
Sun and moon, and stars of light,
Lord of all to thee we raise
This our hymn of grateful praise.

For the joy of ear and eye,
For the heart and mind's delight,
For the mystic harmony
Liking sense to sound and sight,
Lord of all, to thee we raise
This our hymn of grateful praise.

For the joy of human love,
Brother, sister, parent, child,
Friends on earth, and friends above,
For all gentle thoughts and mild,
Lord of all to thee we raise
This our hymn of grateful praise.

For each perfect gift of thine,
To our race so freely given,
Graces human and divine,
Flowers of earth and buds of heaven,
Lord of all to thee we raise
This our hymn of grateful praise.

For thy Church that evermore
Lifteth holy hands above,
Offering up on every shore
Her pure sacrifice of love.
Lord of all to thee we raise
This our hymn of grateful praise.[2]

Notes

1   Blessed John Henry Newman, *Sermons on Subjects of the Day*, Sermon 20.
2   Based on F. S. Pierpoint (1835-1917), 'For the Beauty of the Earth'.

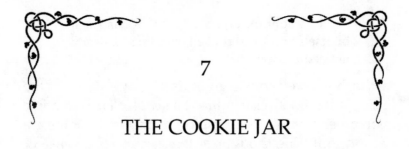

7

THE COOKIE JAR

jingle from an old commercial said that 'Nothing says lovin' like something from the oven.' There is much truth in that expression. That which comes from the oven usually brings love, comfort, hope and affirmation to the recipients. In *The New York Times Bread and Soup Cookbook*, Yvonne Young Tarr tells us:

> Baking is not an art, it is an act of creation. This is not to say that the baker is an artist, for again, baking is not an art. But in the act of creating a bread, an honest loaf, an object with a presence, a fragrance, a substance, a taste, some would say even a soul, the baker has changed grain and flour and liquid into an entity. She or he has taken yeast, a dormant colony of living plants, and released and nurtured them in embryonic warmth, has sprinkled in sugar on which yeast thrives, has sifted in flour that builds the cellular elastic structure that holds the tiny carbon dioxide bubbles that raise the framework of the house called bread. And in that house is love, and warmth, and nourishment, and comfort and care, and caring, and taking care, and time gone by, and time well spent, and things natural and things good, and honest toil, and work without thought of reward, and all of those things once had, now

lost in a country and a world that has rushed
by itself and passed itself, running, and never
noticed its loss.[1]

A freshly baked cookie gives us a bit of joy just for the
sake of the goodness in life. The cookie jar is a magic
container. Some of the happiest memories of home are
found in it. The thought of that jar brings a sense of
security, peace and comfort. It can be the depository
for extra change, be treasured for its design and
sentiment, be a reminder to bake something for a good
cause, hold a family's little treasures or be the storage
bin for bills. If it is filled with good things to eat, it can
be the source of temptation for children, especially
before meals. Best of all it can be filled with glorious
cookies! Every home should have a large cookie jar!

Cookies make anything festive, from a little girl's
tea party to a big holiday gathering. Moms and their
children bake Christmas cookies together. Mothers
guide little hands in the mixing, rolling, and cutting of
cookies into stars, bells, Christmas trees and other
Christmas designs. This activity can be a big mess, but
the kids love it, especially when they can put the
cookies in old coffee cans, wrap the cans with Christmas paper, and give them as gifts to their friends and
teachers. The wonder and playfulness of a child is
rediscovered in a mother who bakes goodies with her
children. It can also be a time of mom's letting go of
her preoccupations, so she can give full attention to
her helpers in the kitchen. Often when a mother does
something with her children, it is an opportunity for
the children to talk about family situations they do not
understand or a problem they have. A baking activity
is a bonding agent. It is a time to build trust and
uncover a child's need to talk. The parent listens, while

quietly working with the child. Baking cookies and listening are also activities used by therapists and their patients. This can be a happy occasion that gives a lift to the daily hospital routine as well as being a learning situation for the patient. Years ago, in elementary and high schools, many stories can be told about teachers baking things with their students.

Indeed, cookies can make any occasion festive. Our Church has a rich liturgical calendar of memorials, feasts and solemnities. The changing seasons and saint's days are excellent times to create or find new baking delights. Food that represents the liturgical life of the Church can be a part of our meals: pancakes on the Tuesday before Ash Wednesday, simple meals during Lent, hot cross buns on Good Friday, a food from a saint's home or adopted country, a holy card or homemade bit of information about a family member's name day next to one's plate at the main meal or table decorations to mark different seasons of the liturgical year. A basket of bible verses from which each child reads and interprets, or a parent reading the Sunday gospel are only two of the myriad of creative ways to spruce up the kitchen and dining area and add elements of inspiration and education to the gathering. Our liturgy gives us endless opportunities to be inventive through celebrations in our home.

Standing Tall

'She's a tough cookie' is a commonly heard phrase which means nobody pushes this person around or tries to deceive her. Tough cookies are necessary in this society of advanced consumerism, artificiality, confusion, and media influence. Baubles, bubbles, glitter and glamour of the superfluous set influence many people. Women who follow Christ must have a firm wall of resistance so that whatever is popular at the moment does not affect the wisdom of the ages that is only to be found in Jesus. The gentleman bishop, and doctor of the Church, Francis de Sales wrote: 'Avoid all affectation and vanity, all extremes and frivolity. As far as possible keep always to the side of simplicity and modesty, for this is undoubtedly beauty's greatest ornament.'[2]

The woman with a strong contemplative dimension is ever watchful that her loved ones are not hurt by toxic relationships or used as sex objects. Wolves in sheep's clothing, with lustful eyes and clever plots, lurk almost everywhere. However, those with eyes to see clearly are in the know. Real women do not need cleavage. Neither do they wear clothes that are skin tight or have high hems, use excessive make up or commonly display elaborate hair styles. Such customs tarnish the beauty of true femininity. There is nothing lovely about vulgarity or profanity coming from a woman's mouth (children can repeat things at the most inappropriate times). Profane speech adds to our culture of fear and violence and deteriorates the fiber of our society already frayed by moral decline.

There is a whole lot more to a woman than the way she looks. A genuine woman is attractive without tinsel town augmentation or use of in vogue speech. Her identity is not based on how glamorous she is, her spouse, job, clothes, bank account or any other external entity. Her identity comes from the inside and is based on strong inner values and a self worth that is grounded in God. With the help of God, she calls by name what is good and what is evil. She has established boundaries and knows how to say no. Genuine women are not afraid to be countercultural when aspects of the culture are contrary to the teachings of Christ and his Church. A woman's clothes, speech and behavior should not be the cause of unfavorable attention or comment. Many women are held in bondage by the evils in our society. They have protective walls around them because they have been abused, used, betrayed, or been told they were loved just to curry favors or things. They have made bad choices from guilt, shame or other negative reasons. Walls may provide a sense of security but they keep out good things.

Authentic women know they are uniquely loved by God and love him in return. God's love is beyond any definition available. God loves us. No one can love us the way God loves us. Only God can fully satisfy the desire for love within our hearts. We learn to love him more as we grow in his wisdom and grace. All women need to take a few moments each day and do nothing but bask in the reality that they are loved by God. If distractions come, use them to be led back to God's love. If the evil one tempts, say 'Oh, its you again' and turn back to God's love. It matters not whether we feel we are immersed in the ocean of God's love, or if we do not feel a drop of it, we continue to be loved and to love him. Our love is not based on how we perceive or how we mentally grasp God's love. Experiencing his love is a great consolation. However, in his mysterious plan we can mature spiritually better and stronger without consolations. We love God for himself more than for his gifts. When we truly believe we are uniquely loved by God, we can say: I am a woman of God. I am loved by him and I live for him in the responsibilities and duties of my life. Teresa of Avila,

who was never one to mince words, brings it all home
for us.

> Oh, when a soul is hid in thee
> For what adventure can it yearn
> Save love and still more love to learn,
> And thus to love increasingly,
> So deep does love within it burn?
> My God, I pray thee for a love
> That yearns until I see thy face,
> And builds itself a nest above
> Within its true abiding place.[3]

Indeed, mystic women belong to God and are answerable to him. We conduct ourselves so that we are treated with dignity and respect. It is better to be known by beauty of character than beauty of body. Women are a mystery. A sign and safeguard of mystery is modesty. True beauty radiates from the soul more than from the body. Eventually physical beauty fades into dust. Soul beauty is anchored in Christ's truth and can grow as one ages. Soul beauty is visible in a demeanor that is Christ like in word and deed. A tasteful, tidy mode of dress and a clean, neat appearance tells more about a person than most words.

As mystic women we know how important social sensitivity is as a positive attribute. We try to express and protect what we believe without infringing on the rights of, or hurting others. We are available to find help for others who seek that which transcends the social milieu of life. We are alert regarding how statements made by ourselves and others are received in a social gathering. Good manners are a means of extending respect to others, from unusual family members to scruffy strangers. Self control under pressure is shown by courtesy and respect. To hold our tongue can take some doing. To speak the truth graciously requires diplomacy. It is not easy to over-look hurtful slights and mean spirited insults. We strive to be patient and accept the trials and hardships of life with a mature faith and trust in God's Provi-dence. Each time we bypass instant gratification, like holding our tongue from saying sharp words, our character becomes stronger.

Interiorly, we seek and long for truth to take root in our interactions with others. Truth is the foundation on which all things that are stable and dependable rest. To live out the splendor of truth is to live in love. Love rejoices in God's truth which protects and preserves human freedom. If we live in true freedom we are free from the gods of greed, excess, and all other manner of evil. If true freedom prevailed, everyone in the human family will be cared for and respected.

My Word is my Bond

Honest and transparent goodness is easily noticeable in the person who is growing in prayer and in virtue. If we are honest with ourselves, there is no significant gap between how we act and what we feel, between what we say and what we do. Honesty is void of duplicity, pretense and pious trivialities and keeps us out of a lot of trouble. It really is the best policy. We are honest when we actively confront and change ourselves, and see others as they are and not how we perceive or would like them to be. Honesty is not easy, but it is the focus of an honorable and upright life, a noble heart and a clear conscience. Nothing will break a confidence as quickly as a prevarication. It is truly regrettable that lying is almost commonplace in our society. Habitual lies are signs of cowardice because they are used to cover a fault or a mistake, or used to hurt another person. People who lie are afraid to let others really know who they are, or they are afraid to face the consequences of their deeds. Truth requires courage. We acknowledge and respect the facts even if they are unpleasant. When truth is behind the decisions we make, it gives us the quiet courage and calm strength to stand by these decisions in the face of hindrance, opposition, controversy or criticism.

Women who are Christ centered are braver than they think and do not back down in the face of evil. The truthful woman takes what she promises seriously. If promises are made with little thought, or used as an automatic reply, it is easy to make them and then forget them. We should not make promises we cannot keep. When explaining something, wise women know that to speak the truth does not mean that one has to tell every detail. There are many things that are better left unsaid. This is prudence. It is better to keep silence then to speculate or hurt others. To strive to speak truth with a soft and gentle tone and to think twice before we speak brings Christian harmony to the home. What can be more soothing than a woman's voice? Kind words are like a fragrant scent that fills the house. Anyone who speaks gentle, encouraging words can sooth a troubled heart or quiet an anxious mind. She who plants courtesy harvests friendship; she who sows kindness reaps love. Mystic women have a unique spiritual perspective. They know life is short and it needs to be lived well, because each person is ultimately accountable to God for his or her behavior. Mystics sense a deep hunger or brokenness present in people's souls and in society. In small and quiet ways, women help to fill the emptiness and longing in those who desire more than what the current trends in society have to offer.

When looking at the history of humanity, John Paul II said 'Women have contributed to that history as much as men, and more often than not they did so in much more difficult circumstances... to this great, immense feminine 'tradition' humanity owes a debt which can never be repaid.'[4] He described women as 'The symbol of God's tenderness toward the human race.'[5] He continued to say 'Our time in particular awaits the manifestation of that genius which belongs to women and which can ensure sensitivity for human beings in every circumstance.'[6] Teresa of Avila guides us:

> You must not build upon foundations of prayer and contemplation alone, for unless you strive after the virtues and practice them, you will never grow to be more than dwarfs. God grant that nothing worse than this may happen — for, as you know, anyone who fails to go forward, begins to go back, and love, I believe, can never be content to stay for long where it is.[7]

Mystics put Jesus' words into action. These actions do not invite people to muse about the fluffy daydreams in their heads, but encourage them to ponder the real issues in life and appropriately use their gifts and talents for the betterment of life.

Family: A Mighty Fortress

Integrity of the soul is manifest in a sound self respect and a strong sense of dignity. A Christian home is a special sanctuary, a refuge from the evil and nonsense of the world. The Christian way of life opposes many things that are popular today. A wife and mother asks: As a unit what does my family stand for in this world? The Christian family is called to be Christ's witness in the world no matter what the responses of the world may be. This is a demanding task. It takes great courage to go into the world as disciples of Christ, be his voice for love and truth and thereby bring about the kingdom of God. The great test of society is the way it understands and treats human life, especially the lives of the preborn, the newborn, the disabled, the gravely ill, the elderly and other marginalized people. The first concern of life should be the caring for life itself. Authentic feminism values motherhood and family life. The vocation of marriage is a positive investment in the future of society. A husband and wife's openness to love and life strengthens their respect for each other, their self control, their unity as a family, and thereby sustains love and life in the country in which they live. Parents give their children roots to know where home is, and wings to fly away and practice what is learned there.

The woman is the heart of the family. The birth of each one of her children is the highest and most miraculous manifestation of God's creative love. Human development between the time of conception and the time of birth is the most miraculous process, and is the fastest and most complex period of growth, in the human life span. By the miraculous actions of God and the ingenuity of a woman's reproductive system, the wife brings forth a child from her womb. In earlier times, a pregnancy was called being with child. A mother once said 'When I think about how I love my children, I sometimes feel I have a window into the heart of God.' The family is a child's first church, first school, first place of refuge. The family, consisting of husband, wife, their offspring, grandparents, aunts, uncles, cousins and other extended or blended family members, mold and shape the children born to it as no other influence in this world. A Christian family illustrates how feeding, clothing, educating and sheltering go hand in hand with self discipline, responsibility, and Christian morals and values. Parents have the most awesome task there is: preparing their children to live with the realities of life and putting them on the road that will take them to heaven. Often this is a call to do not what parents would like to do, but to do what is right in the eyes of God. Parents are the most powerful and best influence on their children. They are the clarion voice for their children. Children tend to do what their parents do and value what their parents value. Seeing parents pray at home, worship in church, be faithful to their responsibilities, act kindly toward each other and others, maintain good nutritional habits, and engage in wholesome recreational activities leaves a lasting mark. Their good example also effects children outside of the family unit more than can be imagined.

The time for family prayer is not an escape from the world. When families pray, they hold their problems and the world's problems in their hands and by that, see the world in a different way. There is a shift in focus from individual wants to societal needs. Steadfast prayer gives families the courage to profess what they believe, and stand up for what they profess. Just because everybody is doing it, or wearing it, or owning it, does not make it right. Christian mystics call others to live the Church's teachings wholeheartedly. There is no 'pick and choose' mentality here. A mother sticks with daily prayer even though it is the last thing she wants to do. Prayer and faith are not lived as if one were in a cafeteria line choosing the most favorite of foods. If a person's religious diet is only of favorite items, it has gross deficiencies. The Church has preserved a spiritual banquet of wisdom since the time of Christ. If people pick the foods from this banquet that only appeal to their spiritual appetite at the moment, it won't nourish them for the journey on the long road of life. If they feast upon the spiritual bonbons popular at this time and in this culture, they will starve their souls. What is currently in vogue usually leaves a lot to be desired. Meals at the Twinkie drive-through at the 'church of what's happening now' are very low in nutrition and short term in substance. Faith is not a matter of random choices or individual reasoning; it is a matter of loving and living the truths of Christ and his Church.

More Love to Give

There are many kinds of cookies on the baking sheet of life. Like the people we know, cookies vary in size and shape, color and texture, appearance and content. They can be half baked, burned to a crisp or just right. There are cookies that make us happy and cookies we do not particularly like. Ethnic cookies remind us of our homeland and dear relatives. Eating an abundance of delectable Christmas cookies during the holidays is balanced with eating healthy cookies in ordinary time. Many times cookies are like people: sweet, spicy, fruity, nutty, hard, soft, simple or complex. Whether home made or store bought, cookies are an all time favorite treat.

There is a special gift in life that is much more than a treat. It is based on being loved, but more importantly, on having the ability to give love. Catherine de Vinck said 'Friendship is a basket of bread from which to eat for years to come. Good loaves fragrant and warm miraculously multiplied; the basket is never empty and the bread never stale.'[8] Friends are like bread recipes. Some come and go like recipes we tried and liked for awhile. Other friends are like rare, treasured recipes that we keep for a lifetime. Sound friendships grow slowly and steady, and withstand the storms of adversity and pain. Teresa of Avila knew about the blessings that come from having spiritual friends. She said 'What a great favor God does to those whom he places in the company of good people.' Indeed, spiritual friends are like rare diamonds in the cookie jar of life.

Friends are like stars in the sky and among them are a few who shine most brilliantly. They are our spiritual friends. Even when a spiritual friend is not present, thoughts of him or her can lift us out of the doldrums. A spiritual friend is an authentic soul mate in Christ and is always held in our hearts and in our prayers. Spiritual friends keep each other dear in prayer. Prayer is their sacred bond and their sacred trust. Precious is the friendship that has its roots in Jesus and deepens with his love. Attentive love centers on that which is most cherished. The silence and solitude in our day gives us the opportunity to have a greater capacity for, and deeper appreciation of, our spiritual friends. The more we are united to God, the closer we become to dear friends. Love is found most profoundly in silence and solitude. This isn't the surface love that causes us to dance around in the happiness of the present moment, but rather the deep down love that sustains and supports us throughout our lives. Deep down love overflows and enhances our family life, and sanctifies the ordinary aspects of our days. Silence and solitude are like deep reservoirs which always remind us of how God is mysteriously working at the present moment. Only by deeply descending into our own hearts and finding God there, are we able to deeply share the good and bad elements of our lives with a few spiritual friends. Silence and solitude with God give us a beautiful contemplative connection with our genuine soul friends.

Spiritual friends are rare and beautiful beyond description. Friends of this caliber are the ones with whom we can share our strengths, weaknesses, joys, trials, innermost thoughts, frightening experiences, fragility and vulnerability without being fearful. Spontaneity and transparency strengthens the friendship and helps it to grow in God. We let the friend know who we really are, even though we know that sharing deeply has its risks. We are not afraid to express our deep doubts, fears, hopes and dreams. We are receptive as we share open conversation and reflective quiet. Personal disclosure and mutual sharing with a beloved friend often clarifies and confirms our own thoughts.

Silence and solitude nurture the tap root of humility in our lives. Humility is an essential nutrient that keeps spiritual friendships growing. Spiritual friends enjoy special benefits, but they are very aware of human flaws. With humility the little rifts and miffs that come along are quickly mended and healed. Even spiritual friendships are not perfect. We still have our weak spots, delicate sensitivities and selfish ways. Humility, ever at work within us, increases our knowledge of self as rooted in Christ and deepens these roots through habitual reconciliation. Humility brings us to the doors of divine mercy, on which we knock frequently, and continue to be fascinated by the goodness and love of God. Indeed, our own weaknesses, limitations and quirks are sources for learning, compassion and wisdom. We become more concerned about the well being of our friend than we are of our own. Feelings and views are truly respected. Failings and faults are easily forgiven. A sacred contentment is experienced when talking about topics from the humorous to the serious, or when sitting in silence and just being together. The bonding between soul friends goes beyond thoughts and words. It is the most beautiful gift we can give and receive. We know we are cherished when so much we do is taken for granted. We are heard when we are not really sure of what we want to say. We are treasured when we doubt our worth. The exploration of this singular gift of spiritual friendship is an unfolding manifestation of lasting inner beauty and eternal values. It transcends sickness, old age and death, and comes to full bloom in heaven.

Solitude pours the waters of grace into intimacy. Deep sharing develops from deep solitude. We grow in prayer and in our friendship with God in silent solitude. We grow in vulnerability and in trust with a good friend who is on our spiritual wave length. Growth in prayer and in friendship is often painful. When there are no distractions in our moments of God centered solitude and silence, we experience deep love and gratitude for the blessed and bittersweet beauty in prayer and in friendship. Pain fosters growth and is a part of prayer. Many times we pray for our spiritual friend at the foot of the cross. Prayer never ceases to astonish us. C. S. Lewis had an extraordinary friendship with his wife Joy. When she was dying of cancer Lewis said: 'I pray all the time these days. If I stopped praying, I think I'd stop living.' 'And God hears your prayer, doesn't he?' the chaplain replied. 'We hear Joy's getting better.' 'Yes,' Lewis replied, but he explained: 'That's not why I pray, Harry, I pray because I can't help myself. I pray because I'm helpless. I pray because the need flows out of me all the time, waking and sleeping. Prayer doesn't change God. It changes me.'

Intimacy has been described as being at home with someone. This holds true for being at home with God, with ourselves and with those whom we hold dear. Intimacy is a costly pearl, but well worth the price. We find intimacy by being good friends with ourselves and diving deep into the mysteries of our lives before we can risk intimacy with God and with others. Although we pay a great price for the intimacy of love, it helps us grow beyond what we ever imagined. Indeed, one of the great rewards in life is to be able to love and to tell those whom we love that we love them. We learn to love from Jesus. He loves us beyond description. He walks beside us and is our best of friends. St Columba sings of his love in his beautiful Celtic hymn:

> The King of Love my Shepherd is,
> Whose goodness fails me never;
> I nothing lack if I am his,
> And he is mine forever.

> Where streams of living water flow
> With gentle care he leads me,
> and where the verdant pastures grow
> With heav'nly food he feeds me.

> Perverse and foolish I have strayed
> But yet in love he sought me,

And on his shoulder gently laid,
And home, rejoicing brought me.

In death's dark vale I fear no ill
With you, dear Lord, beside me,
Your rod and staff my comfort still,
Your Cross before to guide me.

You spread a table in my sight,
Your saving grace bestowing;
And O what joy and true delight
From your pure chalice flowing!

And so through all the length of days
Your goodness fails me never;
Good Shepherd, may I sing your praise
Within your house forever.[9]

Teresa's friendship with Jesus meant everything to her. Her other friendships were various expressions of her great friendship with Christ. Jesus longs to give himself to us, but he does so only to the measure that we genuinely strive to give ourselves to him. Friendships in the Lord are like sturdy golden supports that are woven into the fabric of our lives. These friends give us quiet strength when we are frayed or frazzled. They may give us some advice or suggestions but the strength of the friendship is that it is centered in Jesus. As sentinels and guardians of our souls, spiritual friends stand by our side. To be able to share the loose ends and the mysteries in our lives is a precious and great blessing. Friends in the Lord divide our sorrow and double our joy. Their presence is like a sweet, healing balm on an open wound of the heart. Many times their supportive quiet means more than a babble of words. Friends stay with us when the chips are down. When we are bone weary, confused, depressed or deep in a dark night of the soul the friend is there. When we are enthusiastic, at peace, happy as a clam, or radiant with hope, the friend is there. A faithful friend is a shelter in the storm, a playmate in wonderland and most of all, a sunbeam that keeps us on the path to God.

There is no way we can sustain intimacy without the cross. Because whatever causes us to suffer can shrink us or stretch us; we always have to make a choice. We have seen people who have suffered, or who are suffering, become hard and bitter with constant cries of sorrow. Oh what a sad life is a constant refrain as they woefully sing the blues. On the other hand, we have seen people whose suffering is met with simple acceptance, quiet adjustments and whose limitations are a challenge from which to learn. They have a cheerful countenance and are a joy to be around. Their melodies are happy with hope. Indeed, that which makes us suffer can be a curse or a blessing. There are many examples of how a handicapped child can pull members of a family apart or draw them together. The power of grace transforms suffering into a redemptive response. United with the crucified Christ, suffering becomes a path to victory because the passion of Christ continues in his mystical body the Church. Together with Jesus we are rooted in a goodness deeper than the worst suffering. With Jesus by our side we can find small graces in the most evil of adversities. With Jesus we offer our sufferings to God for the good of our families, our Church and our world.

Spiritual intimacy which we have with the Triune God and with our spiritual friends, haunts the soul. We are led to strange places. We become more than a specific time in our lives, the temporal limits of our bodies or minds, our accomplishments, our jobs, our achievements or our personal concerns. The risk that is part of intimacy removes the protective fences we build around us or around others. As a great teacher, intimacy brings to the surface God's deep design within us. What we achieved, earned or owned brought us happiness for a time, but it left us with a restlessness and a yearning for something more. Secular accomplishments do not give the tranquil inner peace that comes from deeply knowing God and a few others who are on our spiritual path. Edith Stein tells us: 'To partake of the life of another, to share in everything that concerns him, the largest and the smallest, joy and sorrow, but also work and problems—that is a gift, that is happiness.'

Yes, we pass through times of joy and sorrow on our life's journey, it seems the sorrowful times are etched deeper in our memories. A Gaelic proverb puts it another way: 'A whole day's rapture is soon forgotten, but a sigh in the night lingers long in the ear and heart.' What an astounding blessing it is to be able to share those sighs in the night with a beloved person.

Indeed, we are made by God for him and he is our ultimate satisfaction. The love we have for Jesus Christ is the greatest and strongest bond we share with our spiritual friends. The love we have for God and for our spiritual friends strengthens the love we have for others. God is within us and he is love. Therefore, the depth to which we love others is the depth to which we love God. When we realize this, we begin to imitate Christ by loving him more than anything else in the world. Looked upon with reverence, offered with trust and accepted with grace, intimacy is a mutual gift which evokes wonder, delight, gratitude and awe. To live intimacy is to reflect the life of Jesus Christ by

living fully, serving graciously and loving deeply.
With him we live for love, in love and with love.

Like a Pebble Dropped in a Pond

Each person is unique, a separate being in his or her
own right with his or her own needs and dreams. We
know quite well that true love is far beyond hearts,
flowers, or a warm, cozy feeling. It requires courageous
choices and sacrifices in order for it to be real. Love
begins at home, right now. It is made real by insignificant acts of kindness and sacrifices right where we live.
We will what is good for those around us and provide
it if we are able. What is good for a person is not
necessarily saying something that makes him or her
happy or giving something that is popular at the
moment. It is providing an environment that fosters self
discipline. We work for the sake of those we love rather
than spending time on a continuum of personal pursuits. We tend to a sick child instead of going to the
mall. Sacrifice is not a pious idea; it is a lived reality.
Because it is other centered rather than self centered,
we learn to serve without the need for reciprocation.
This is evident in helping a parent, spouse or child,
when he or she is unable to recognize who is helping.
To truly love is to serve in silence. The grace of God
becomes an indescribable quality and a sustaining
strength to us when we carry on without inner grumbles or external recognition and no signs of gratitude
day after day and year after year. We may not realize
it often, but there is a social and spiritual dimension to
our small individual private acts of love. By offering
our prayer, care, sacrifices, hardships and difficulties to
God, they improve the atmosphere of the area in which

we work, as well as the atmosphere of the society in which we live.

Someone wrote these words a long time ago: Love is giving with no thought of receiving. It is tenderness unfolding with strength to protect humankind. It is forgiveness without dwelling on what was forgiven. It is forgiveness repeated freely throughout a lifetime. It is understanding human weakness, and knowing unique beauty lies underneath. It is quiet in the midst of turmoil. It is trust in God with no thought of self. It is the glory in sacrifice and the ultimate wonder and mystery of God. It is the light in a mother's eyes, the quiet assurance of a father's protection, the glory in sacrifice, the fragility and innocence of a young child. Love gives hope to others when times are difficult. It extends compassion without condescension, and service without need for appreciation. It liberates our souls, allowing us to breathe the purified air of faith and teaches us how to rest in God when we are experiencing the mysteries of suffering. It is the expectation of our Father's promise coming true. It is the refusal to see anything but good in our fellow human beings. It is the glory that comes with selflessness and the power that comes with the awareness of our Father's love for his children. It is the voice that says 'no' to our brother or sister, parent or child, though 'yes' might be more easily said. It is resistance to the world's lust and greed, thus becoming a light in the presence of error.

Love is the one thing no one can take from us. Love is the one thing we can give constantly and become increasingly rich in the giving. Love is the one thing that is repaid by love alone. Love can take no offense, for it cannot know that which it does not itself contain. It cannot hurt or be hurt for it is the purest reflection of God. It is the one eternal indestructible force for good. It is the will of God preparing, planning, proposing, always what is best for all his people.

> Father we thank you for your love and your many blessings, especially the precious gift of each other. Help us to show our gratitude by loving each other as you loved us. Make us understanding and patient with one another, quick to admit our failings and ask forgiveness, generous in sharing the joy and strength we can give each other. Father, give our family lively faith and the courage to share it with those around us. Direct us to the state in life you plan for each of us and help us to use your gifts to serve you. We entrust our family to your fatherly care. Preserve us from the corruption of the modern world and help us draw closer daily to you and to each other, until we come to share with you the joys of heaven. Jesus, Mary and Joseph, help us to be a holy family. Amen.

Notes

1   See Y. Young Tarr, *New York Times Bread and Soup Cookbook* (New York: Quadrangle/New York Times Book, 1972).

2   St Francis de Sales, *Introduction to the Devout Life*, 25.

3   St Teresa of Avila, Poem IV: 'Si el amor que me tenéis'.

4   Pope John Paul II, *Letter to Women* (1995), 3.

5   Idem, *Vita consacrata* (1996), 57.

6   Idem, *Mulieris dignitatem* (1988), 30.

7   St Teresa of Avila, *Interior Castle*, Seventh Mansions, chapter 4, 13.

8   Paraphrase of C. de Vinck, 'Children of a New Season' in *A Time to Gather: Selected Poems* (Allendale, NJ: Alleluia Press, 1974), p. 58.

9   The hymn, based on Psalm 23, was written by Henry W. Baker (1821–1877), and the tune frequently used is known as St Columba.

WHEN THE CUPBOARD IS BARE

The day began like most other days. Nothing in the morning air hinted at what was to come. There were no unusual colorings in the sunshine outside of Beth's kitchen window, there was no hint of disaster in the wind. It was a clear day, as Beth recalled it now; sunny and filled with the color of autumn: October 17th. Even now she cringes as she writes that date. Beth had arrived home from a trip two days earlier. On her kitchen table was a deep red rose which had been given to her in welcome by Mike, her husband of thirty years. 'Welcome home! I love you!' read the card, still resting just below the small glass vase. The penmanship was so familiar, as was everything else about this man Beth had known and loved for well over half of her life. 'I know your face better than I know my own,' she said to him recently. Her own face was seen only in photos, or backwards in a mirror. Mike's face, however, was the one she saw day after day. It is safe to say that she took that face for granted, for it would always be there. That bearded, smiling face with its oddly dimpled nose and what she called 'blue and amber eyes' would always be there to laugh, tease, comfort, pray, sometimes disagree, and always love...

On this bright October morning, Mike and Beth decided to go out for breakfast. After all, it was a Saturday and she had just returned from a trip. Both of their sons, young men in their twenties, were out hiking. Mike and Beth went to Mike's favorite breakfast restaurant. Over his plate of sausage and eggs, he looked at Beth solemnly and said 'Don't leave again anytime soon—I miss you too much.' Perhaps inspired by this proclamation, on the way home Beth said to him: 'If I had the chance to marry you all over again, I'd do it even more quickly now.' As she looked back, she believed these words were inspired.

They hadn't been home long when it happened. Mike was busy working on a project in the back of the house. Beth was in the family room copying a videotape she had filmed on her trip. Knowing that Mike wanted to tape a football game, she hurriedly finished her little project and then went to tell him the machine was free for his use. She went toward the back of the house calling to him...

And the world she had known was gone. There was no answer to her calls. What happened next cannot be recalled except in jagged fragments. Mike lying unresponsive on the floor. Beth running out the front door, remembering that a neighbor knew CPR. She was dialing 911. She was sent from neighbor to neighbor. A man stood in her house calling 'Mike! MIKE!' A woman she had never met was running up her street. Beth tried desperately to follow her, but her legs were strangely weighted with lead. Her mouth had turned into cotton, and although she could not form words she was crying aloud: 'God, please don't take him! Mike, you know I need you! Please, please don't go!' Her lead legs reached her front landing and as her foot thudded onto the bottom step she said aloud '...but God, your will, not mine, be done...'

The sound of sirens. An ambulance. Beth was making a desperate phone call: 'Please pray!' A neighbor was loading Beth into a car to follow the ambulance. 'He still has a mild heartbeat,' she was saying, and Beth clung to this news as to a life raft. The hospital. Ushered into a little room. Three friends had all arrived before her, alerted by her call for prayer. Her pastor sat there saying 'your neighbor Tom called me,' and she knew she had no neighbor named Tom. A doctor in the little room, telling her 'You'd better sit down... we did all we could do...' and she thought wildly 'It's just like they say on TV...' It was a dream. Beth knew it was a dream. She would wake up soon and see those blue and amber eyes and she would say 'You'll never believe what I just dreamed...' But it was real, too. So horribly real. A neighbor came in crying, the neighbor who knew CPR, and said 'if only I'd been there!' and Beth said 'You can't stay home just because somebody may need CPR...' Someone told Beth she must go in and see her husband and Beth said firmly 'no.' She could not see him lifeless. She could not face him if he wouldn't talk to her. That might make this awful dream come true.

They made her go in. 'You have to,' the hospital chaplain insisted. They wound up dragging her, for she could no longer walk. She could no longer think, no longer breathe, no longer be, because time had split. He was there then, so terribly there. So still. Somehow Beth sat down beside him. Somehow she found the breath to speak and words poured into a flood: 'I will always love you, I forgive you for not losing weight, I'm sorry for everything I ever did to hurt you, I will always love you, I forgive everything you ever did or said that bothered me, I will always love...'

Time Splits

Sometimes in life, everything is undone. Our most beloved one dies, our great projects collapse. Our home burns to the ground, we lose our job, life savings, memory or our ability to speak. Our intuitions or new discoveries become meaningless. It seems like we are frozen in time or going backward.

The road of life is full of curves. Sometimes they come one at a time and sometimes in rapid succession. Going around a bend that ends in loss is part of life, and it is never easy. This curve can find us totally unaware, somewhat prepared or somewhere in between.

Each loss is different. Each contains mourning which we must acknowledge and work through. The process of mourning is unique to the situation and to the person experiencing it. People also differ in the time it takes to integrate a loss. Mourning, like looking at a particular work of art or reading a specific book, affects each person differently according to his or her make up. No two persons respond the same way to the same type of loss. We are different in temperament, character, values, endurance and circumstances surrounding the loss.

In time and with God's help we learn to accept the painful realities of loss. This can be the most difficult thing we have ever done. Because each loss varies in its impact upon us, we change in our capacity to adjust. Major losses have profound effects we never anticipated. Minor losses cause disturbances beyond our expectations. As the certainty of loss settles in, we face its reality, grow with its pain and get on with our lives. If we do not face our pain, somewhere it will wait for us. We cannot continue to deny it through over work, addictions or any other escape route. Integrating loss is a slow and difficult process. We grow in our trust in God and rely on help in ways we never dreamed. We may seem the same on the outside to others, but on the inside we are different. We grasp at straws when we try to explain how we are different. More often than not, it is something beyond spoken words as well as beyond our thoughts.

A life crisis has the power to stimulate spiritual development. Spiritual development is the highest and most important of our developmental areas. It sustains us with grace that enables us to live with paradox, conflict and unanswered questions. For the spiritually mature, loss brings significant disturbance on the surface, but the ability to find the peace of God's love at our depths. Peace develops after we learn to live with a habitual, heartfelt yes to God. As a continual challenge that calls us to a greater love, our yes pulls us beyond our self and our immediate situation. Christ is fashioned anew within us when our minds are no longer gripped by thoughts that center on our problematic issues. We observe that the difficult and hostile events of life have another side. That side brings out strength and gifts we never knew we had. At this point we begin to live with the certainty that our trust in God is greater than our problems relating to loss.

The purity of God's love illuminates our resistance, weakness and fear with a new light. We acknowledge and realize what they are doing to us, and strive to let them go. Another slow and agonizing process! However, when we cooperate with the lights from God's grace, that which holds us back loses its power over us. The energy we use in our fear and resistance is overcome by the energy of God's love working in us. Our journey through grief does not depend on us alone. We seek God in our grief, knowing that he seeks us more. His ways of helping us can surprise us. Often, he shows his love for us through the love and concern of others.

Within the mourning context, people who come to our aid can be known to us or can be unexpected strangers. Whoever they are, their care and love will usually come from their experience of wounds and hurts. A gentle recognition and acceptance of their wounds allow them to let go of the things that protected them and move forward with a deeper concern. They know that to share sorrow with another makes it less burdensome and painful. The presence of a person who brings love in this form is one sign of God's hidden presence. The ability to console well is a noble and sensitive art. It develops loss into a channel of growth for ourselves and others. The greater our losses and trust in God, the better our capacity to offer consolation and comfort to others in an appropriate manner. To be with others and walk with them is most important. Talk is secondary because most of the time we do not have the right words to offer, advice to give or solutions to suggest. There is a fine line between being supportive and insensitive. Experience shows us that we rarely bring God to others through our wisdom. More often it is through the mysterious workings of grace. Companioning has a tendency to boomerang. Through the witness of their lives, those who are wounded teach us about God. The gifts of God are found more by walking with someone and sharing

God's wonder, than talking to him or her in a guru like way.

Like the disciples at Emmaus, we must be attentive to seeing Jesus walking with us. God is present in every situation of our lives, but we must look carefully to find him. Many of the painful times in life occurred because we expected something and that something did not turn out the way we expected. God calls us to step forward in faith and trust in the care he gives us through those who love us. We share our vulnerability with others and discover God in our midst. When we let go of trying to fix or change others, we discover deep, beautiful places in their hearts. As we walk with them, we hold their hurting places in our own hearts. Empathy requires much listening. To practice empathy is to turn the key that opens hearts and discovers sanctuaries of peace therein. This peace helps us to give from the deepest recesses of our own hearts. Because we experience the healing love of Jesus, we become signs of the great love God offers us. In time, loss becomes a place to meet God, for he is found everywhere.

It is hard to be open and receptive when we have been wounded and hurt. When pain is raw in its newness, to say that God is with us, or to hold faith up as a support can be difficult. Because our pain is overwhelming, we only see the consuming fact of our loss. God and faith seem distant. It is difficult to hear the good news of faith right after the bad news of major loss.

Dawning

Most of the time, the light from grace does not appear suddenly. It grows in intensity as we persevere in blind trust and prayer. The increase in light may be compared to the sun at its rising. In the gray before dawn only large objects are visible. Details are shadowed and blurred. Misinterpretations are made for want of light. As sunlight approaches, details become more distinct and their importance realized. Much later, the noonday sun reveals all, even the motes in a seemingly clear shaft of light. As the light of grace brightens our inner landscape we are able to focus on Jesus' teachings more clearly and understand them in new ways. One lesson we learn here is that we cannot sympathize with the wretchedness of others until we know the wretchedness within ourselves.

Preoccupation with what grieves us can lead us in two directions. On the positive side we ask: how can we find God in such thoughts? We find him as we pick up the pieces. We see alternatives and opportunities despite our heartache. We avoid focusing on what happened to us, and concentrate on what to do with what happened. We do not give up. On the negative side we become bitter, pessimistic and fear filled because of what we no longer have. We feel cheated, overwhelmed and trapped. We imagine and expect the worst. Such dead end thoughts influence the way we do things. They insulate us from today's world, almost without our knowing it. Negative attachments lead us away from searching for God in a consistent, prayerful way. (This holds true with positive attachments as well.)

Not everything that happens to us has meaning or makes sense. Nevertheless, baffling events and circumstances can be the foundation for discovering God's love and bringing light out of darkness, order out of chaos, meaning out of meaninglessness and life out of death. We need to stop ruminating on things we cannot change, sit back, relax and give God a chance. Violence, accidents, illness, death and other occurrences that wring the heart are not the will of God. God's will is manifest through our choices that are based on love. God restored what was lost by sin and bound by death by sending us Jesus. Nothing can separate us from Christ. God gave us the responsibility to take care of what he created. Yes, we are bewildered by tragic and unexplainable events and circumstances, but God is there. He may seem distant and silent to us, but he is there.

As our loss becomes integrated we learn to live in the present moment. We find joy in who and where we are right now. Although we face future responsibilities and plans, we do not think about the future as the source for our peace and happiness. We live ahead of ourselves if we think our future will bring us more peace and happiness than what we have today. Peace and happiness are not back there where we were, or in front of us waiting for us to arrive. They lie within our hearts and decrease or increase by how we live today. Peace and happiness add to the contentment found with who and where we are here and now. If we look around, we see that the happiest people are those who make the most of the present. They do not look back over their shoulder or look forward to the future. They are fully alive to the present moment.

Catherine of Siena once wrote:

> Make light of the world and of yourself, and of all earthy pleasures. Hold your kingdom as something lent to you, not as if it were your own. For you know well that life, health, wealth, honor, status, dominion—none of these belongs to you. If they did, you could own them

> in your own way. But just when we want to be
> healthy we are sick; just when we want to be
> alive we die; just when we want to be rich we
> are poor; just when we want to be in power we
> are made servants. And all this because these
> things are not ours, and we can keep them only
> as much and as long as it pleases the One who
> has lent them to us. So it is really foolish to hold
> as if it were our own what belongs to another...
> This is why I am asking you to act wisely, as a
> good steward, holding everything as lent to you
> who have been made God's steward.[1]

Nothing in this world belongs to us. Everything we
have is on loan. We strive to be wise stewards who
care for what we have. We are entrusted with the
administration of the gifts of God's creation. The more
we let God into our lives, the more he teaches us about
ways to tend to his gifts. God's love for us is manifest
in our love for what he created. We use what we need
with gratitude and distribute what we do not need to
others according to their needs. We neither squander
the goods entrusted to us nor use them excessively or
carelessly. We use things with care because we know
all good things come from God. We seek him by
showing reverence toward what he has created.

Like a ship that drops unnecessary baggage over the
side, we find that the lighter our load the faster we
travel and the sooner we arrive at the harbor of God.
We hold on to the necessities of life with a light grasp.
Image, power, possessions, success and other so called
signs of prestige in our society are no longer as important as they once were. From a spiritual perspective,
they are illusions that stand in the way of what is real.
The eye blink of life on earth is miniscule compared to
the eternal gaze of heaven. Clinging to people and

things uses up much energy. Manipulating people and owning the latest adult toys requires more time and money than we thought. A reality of life is that we cannot hold onto it or control it. Instead of standing in self acclaimed power, we walk forward as a pilgrim who travels light.

No one said we need to be a success in everything we do. Teresa of Calcutta noted that God did not ask her to be successful, but to be faithful. All we do is plant seeds. We plant the best we know how and leave the rest to God. This is how we are faithful. We do the best we can when we know who we are, what we are capable of, and to whom we belong. As we grow in our knowledge of God we realize who we are is not based on what we accomplish. More importantly, we find who we are at the center of our hearts. The more we see the uniqueness within ourselves, the more we see the uniqueness of others. We no longer expect them to be like us, but give them freedom to find their own distinct identity.

Losses in life are very real, but so is God. When loss becomes part of our lives, we pray, listen, and try to do what we think God wants us to do, one day at a time. God enters into our losses and transforms them by his presence. Yes, God is with us, but different from any way we experienced or expected. We find that hope is not just an optimistic attitude. It is an outlook of mind and heart. In the midst of deep sadness and suffering we know that steadfast love transforms, that change promotes growth, and that conversion of heart continues through prayer and patience. The words of Helen Keller are a source for reflection: 'So much has been given to me, I have no time to dwell on what has been denied.'

Letting go is not a one time experience. It is something we experience and learn from over and over again on different levels. Faith takes on whole new dimensions in the various darknesses of our lives. Faith becomes trust when it looks like there is no future. Faith is a leap in the dark when we start something new. Faith is almost stretched to the breaking point after years and years of toil. When we think our faith in God has come to a dead stop, it hasn't really stopped. It has just changed. The call of faith rings true when we find new belief from dreadful things that happen to us.

Sarah's story

Raising two children alone was not the easiest thing to do but certainly brought me great joy. Money was always tight, yet we seemed to manage. Except one month I needed to stretch the food to last a couple more days. I did not quite make it. All I had left was flour, potatoes, and brown sugar. I made syrup out of brown sugar and water, very flat pancakes out of flour and water and cooked the potatoes. My kids loved it. I was thankful. Yet, the situation grew worse as I had nothing else for them for the rest of the day, or the next. Monday I would be going to work and would have food to bring home. I worked at a restaurant. The boss allowed anyone to take what they wanted from the leftovers at the end of the day. I could have taken more than what I needed, but I just couldn't do that. I had thoughts of bringing extra food home to stock the freezer... I didn't. I only took what was needed. There were others who needed it just as much as me.

Well, now I find myself in a grim situation. I knew God was aware of me. I made sure of that because I had been sending him my pleas for help. I seemed to be totally in peace. I knew somehow all would be fine. There was nothing else for me to do. Just to be still was what I needed to do.

Not long after breakfast, the kids were playing and I was cleaning up the kitchen. A knock on my front door began a wonderful surprise, a great gift from God. Standing on my porch was my neighbor down the street, Mr O'Sullivan. He had a huge box set on my porch. He mentioned to me that he had been with his son yesterday, at a picnic for policemen's families. They had food left over and he asked if I could use any of it. I was amazed. I said 'Sure!!' He asked if I would share it with my neighbor who had three kids. Inside the box were hot dogs, buns, chips, cookies and drinks. My neighbor came over. We divided the food and later on got together and had a glorious picnic in the back yard.

I am so glad Mr O'Sullivan followed the prompting of the Holy Spirit. He could simply have not responded and we would not have had any food. I thank God for Mr O'Sullivan. He died not long after that, but I will never forget him. He is always in my heart.

One thing I have learned and passed on to my now grown children is to keep extra back up food for emergencies. I always keep canned food, crackers, etc. on hand. Also I have learned that as long as people do all they can to help themselves, and cannot do anymore to improve a situation, God is always with them and takes very good care of their needs.

The greatest hardship we have may be the poverty of having good desires we are unable to fulfill, or wanting to love God more and finding ourselves falling short. Few of us are the wives, mothers, homemakers, parishioners or employees we would like to be. It is here where we learn to accept, surrender and let the Holy Spirit work in us. We do our best and let him take over. This is all God asks. At this point faith is no longer based on nice sentiments, sweet words, institutions or elements of religion that makes us feel good. Faith is a blind trust in God. Teresa of Avila said 'All we can do in prayer is to dispose ourselves, the rest is in the power of the Spirit who leads us.'

After 'bare cupboard' experiences, the ordinary seems transformed. We see life in its beauty, joy and importance. We experience transformation in the first day outdoors after a serious illness, the first flowers after a stark winter, realizing our loved one is truly with God, sharing a cup of tea with a friend we haven't seen in ages, standing in front of a Christmas tree, enjoying a summer's afternoon at the beach, finding tranquility in prayer, and most of all celebrating the Eucharistic Sacrifice. Moments of transformation represent new life, a rebirth which may be felt for a few seconds, several hours, or the rest of our lives. Whatever the length of time, we are touched by the mystery of God in his creation. It is comforting to know that every task, duty and relationship has a transcending dimension. Teresa of Avila comments about our final and greatest time of transformation: 'Life is to live in such a way that we are not afraid to die. Everything seems to me to pass so quickly... that we must concentrate our thoughts on how to die rather than how to live.'

There is a small grave in a large cemetery near a very large international airport. Jets fly over the cemetery in regular intervals ending their journey at the airport. The grave is the earthly resting place of a four year old boy who died quite unexpectedly during a routine operation. On the headstone of the grave is a side view of a little boy in overalls, kneeling as if planting flowers in the earth. By this picture are the words 'Budded on earth to bloom in heaven.' When tragedy crosses our path of life it is a comfort to remember these words. We are all budded on earth to bloom in heaven.

> We seem to give them back to you,
> O God, who gave them to us.
> Yet, as you did not lose them in giving
> so we do not lose them by their return.
> Life is eternal and love immortal
> and death is only a horizon,
> and a horizon is nothing
> except the limit of our sight.
> Lift us up, strong Son of God,
> that we may see further;
> cleanse our eyes
> that we may see more clearly;
> draw us closer to yourself
> that we may know ourselves
> to be nearer to our loved ones
> who are with you.[2]

Notes

1   St Catherine of Siena, *Letter to Charles V, King of France* (August 1376).
2   Prayer attributed to Bede Jarrett OP, 1881–1934. An older version is attributed to Bishop Brent (1862–1926).

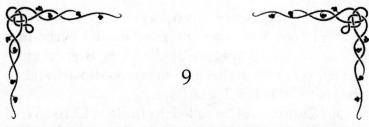

9

THE SOUL AS FEMININE BEFORE GOD

And only where God is seen does life truly begin. Only when we meet the loving God in Christ do we know what life is. We are not some casual and meaningless product of evolution. Each of us is the result of a thought of God. Each of us is willed, each of us is loved, each of us is necessary. There is nothing more beautiful than to be surprised by the gospel, by the encounter with Christ. There is nothing more beautiful than to know him and to speak to others of our friendship with him.[1]

Benedict XVI's words are worth much serious reflective thought. What is more beautiful than knowing Jesus Christ?

Ah, dear feminine soul, what have you to teach us as we bumble down the mystic path? How do we keep you as the most beautiful part of ourselves? While we rest in your garden, what do we do with the beautiful flowers that were sprinkled with the waters of our baptism and whose growth is sustained by our prayer? Indeed, how are we captivated by Christ?

Who is she that most young girls dream about, teenagers hope to be, and for which young ladies prepare? She is a bride. A wedding can be the high point of a young lady's life. It can also be the one most longed for, the most prayed for, the most costly, the most prepared for and the most sacred event in a woman's life. All eyes are drawn to the beauty, grace and happiness of the bride as she walks down the aisle. To be sure, it is her day of days.

Our Church is often called the bride of Christ. What does this mean? Bridal imagery to describe the bond between God and his people has its roots in the Hebrew Scriptures. It was used to distinguish the relationship between God and the people of Israel through the covenant between them. God is the bridegroom of Israel and the people of Israel are the bride. The fifty fourth chapter of Isaiah says: 'For he who has become your husband is your maker; his name is the Lord of Hosts.' In the sixty second chapter he tells us: 'And as a bridegroom rejoices in his bride, so shall your God rejoice in you.' In the Song of Songs, poetic form and expression are used to show the sublime love between God and his people. The Lord is the lover and his people are the beloved. This relationship is described in terms of human love and characterized the covenant between God and Israel in terms of a marriage. God speaks to Israel's heart and renews her as a spiritual people. The author's poem tells us of an ideal Israel who God gently leads to spiritual union with himself by perfect love. The courtship and marriage customs are those from the author's time.

In the Song of Songs, God also calls the soul to make the journey to eternal life. 'Arise, make haste, my love, my dove, my beautiful one, and come; for now the winter has passed, the rains have gone far off, the flowers have appeared in our land, the time of pruning has come, and the voice of the turtledove is heard in our land' (Song of Songs 2:10–12).

In the Christian Scriptures, the theme of Christ as bridegroom was used by John the Baptist. When the people thought that John was the Messiah, he said 'I am not the Messiah, I am sent before him. It is the groom who has the bride. The groom's best man waits there listening for him and is overjoyed to hear his voice. That is my joy and it is complete. He must increase while I must decrease' (John 3: 29–30). John prepared God's people for Jesus. The bride (God's people) is for the bridegroom (Jesus). The bridegroom's friend, (John) hears him and rejoices greatly at Jesus' voice. John's words are for all of us: Jesus' presence within us must increase and for this to happen, our egos must decrease.

After his dramatic conversion on the road to Damascus Paul of Tarsus became the first missionary to spread the good news about Jesus Christ. His travels were prodigious. He wrote many epistles to the Churches that he established in different cities. He was the most dynamic of Christ's apostles and evangelizers. In his letters he made references to the Church as being the spouse of Christ. He preached and wrote about the Church founded by Christ and espoused to Christ. In his letter to the Ephesians, Paul says that a husband is the head of his wife, just as Christ is the head of his body the Church. He tells husbands to love their wives as Christ loves his Church. The bond of Christ and his Church is mystical or espousal. Christ loves the Church like a husband ideally loves his wife. The unity of Christ and his Church is illustrated by the deep personal bond that exists between a bridegroom and his bride so that we can understand the intimate closeness of this union.

The Eucharist is the most intense presence of Christ that there is on this earth. The Eucharist is the spousal gift of Christ himself to his bride, the Church. Jesus referred to himself as the bridegroom in the second chapter of Mark. His apostles spoke of the whole Church, and of each of the faithful, as a bride betrothed to Jesus. This was so that the faithful might become one in spirit with him. In the New Testament, the Church is referred to as the bride of the spotless lamb. Jesus loved his Church to the point of dying for her sanctification. *Verbi Sponsa*, an Instruction on the Contemplative Life states: 'The Son of God presents himself as the Bridegroom Messiah, (who has) come to seal the marriage of God with humanity, in a wondrous exchange of love which begins in the incarnation, comes to its summit of self offering in the passion and is forever given as gift in the Eucharist.'[2]

Shining like the Sun

As the bride is most beautiful to her husband on her wedding day, so must our souls be most beautiful for Jesus our Lord. Oh, how he ravishes the hearts of those who welcome him in. He is closer to us than we can possibly be to ourselves, and is closer to us than any other person can be to us. The degree to which we keep our souls beautiful for Jesus is our choice. We are always striving for the better part of life. We are always thirsting for that which is beautiful. Jesus' wisdom is the only water from love's wellspring that can truly quench our deepest thirst. Teresa of Avila keeps our attention on the right things: 'We know we have souls. But we seldom consider the precious things that can be found in this soul, or who dwells within it, or its high value. Consequently, little effort is made to preserve its beauty. All our attention is taken up with the plainness of the diamond's setting... that is, with these bodies of ours.' She continues 'I knew well that I had a soul, but I did not understand the dignity of this soul, nor did I know who lodged within it, because my eyes were blinded by the vanities of this life, so that I was prevented from seeing him. I think that, had I known then as I do now, that in this little palace of my soul so great a King is lodged, I would not have left him alone so often, but at least sometimes I would have stayed with him and been more careful to prepare a clean lodging for him.'

John of the Cross gives us these very practical words so that we can keep our lodging clean: 'Do not feed your spirit on anything apart from God. Cast away all cares and let peace and reconciliation fill your heart.' The common bond we have as mystics is that we are all sinners. A daily habit of forgiveness and reconciliation is very important for a clean lodging. Mystics are as different as day and night, and when working with others, there are bound to be times of friction. On occasion, mystic women can get upset, grumpy, snappy, angry, out of sorts, or irritated. We can have disagreements, quibbles, spats and heated arguments. We can be rude, stubborn, ill tempered, irksome or a bit eccentric. Peace comes when we control our inordinate behavior. It is consoling to know that after periods of discord, we are able to come together and experience unity and peace.

Struggle in the spiritual life comes in many forms. Experiencing dryness or distractions at prayer is common. Spiritual desolation has been the lot of many great saints. The saints experience this desolation as a gift of sharing in the suffering of Jesus on the cross. At the foot of the cross we see how each mystic is an odd mix of competency and vulnerability, strength and fragility, set priorities and spontaneity. We can be as strong as an ox at times and as weak as a kitten other times. We have faults, some of which are outstanding, and we make mistakes. However, what sets us apart from the common population is that when we fall, we get up and try again. We keep on trying. We know the dangers of complacency and do not even rest on our laurels. We focus on the pros rather than on the cons of life. We are resilient, like a perpetually bouncing ball. We keep the faith and never lose heart or hope. We love God by being faithful to daily prayer and by expressing his love within humanity. This has its creative tensions.

To be rooted in eternity is to not be deceived by political correctness or the pettiness, prejudices and pressures of the day. Speculations and theories about tragedies of the human condition, problems in the Church, or almost any other subject can go on forever. Discussions, dialogues and debates are helpful to a point, but they can only go so far and are not necessary components of faith and religion. Faith and religion can weaken if current cultural values and relativism are emphasized. Let us use sin as an example. Our hedonistic society diminishes or denies the existence of sin. It is easy to give reasons or excuses why we sin. On the other hand we can become morbidly preoccupied with sin. Discussions can also change into intellectual jousts, analytical probes, power trips or other types of verbal exchange.

The energy in our prayer motivates us to do something rather than just talk about sin. God's mercy is real because our sins are real. We take responsibility for our sins. We are truly contrite if we do something to put things right. We atone for our sins by fasting, making sacrifices, and giving of our time and talents. The luminous mercy of God takes us out of our own heads and guides us in the giving of ourselves to others. Because God is ultimate mystery and consummate love, the human mind is unable to fathom him. Faith and religion are decisions that go beyond the knowledge in our individual minds and in the collective mind of various groups. To believe in God is to say yes to the gift of faith. To live the reality and vision of the Catholic Christian is to experience this gift at its most profound and most blessed form.

Common Mysticism

We try to use our time well. Within our daily time frame, we practice saying no to a job instead of doing many jobs poorly because we are spread too thin. There is an art to knowing what is enough regarding our time, energy, money, activities at Church, other organizations to which we belong and even prayer. Are we too involved? We learn to let go of extraneous activities. This takes regular evaluations and hard changes. What are the activities I am involved with and how are they consistent with the God-centered realities in my life? We are always watchful because we never want to become so busy during the day that we forget about God. We cannot be a mystic without a deep prayer life. Rarely is something so important that we need to give up prayer. If we give up prayer, we have been tricked by the evil one. We are not 'busy bee' women, we are gospel women. We live the gospel by our good behavior more than by how many good things we do. The ordinary behavior of mystic women in the Church should command such respect that it ennobles others and directs them to the heart of Christ. Benedict XVI urges us on: 'Women are also the first doors to the Word of God in the Gospel, they are authentic evangelists... who always help us to know the word of God, not only through their intelligence, but also through their hearts.'[3]

Experiencing the ordinary in prayer is also a mark of the mystic. It is said that receiving one holy communion with steadfast love has a much greater value than visions, locutions. levitations, bilocations, ecstasies or other unusual experiences that are not naturally possible. This is most certainly true. Extraordinary mystical experiences and uncommon behavior are not needed or required on our journey toward God. Neither are they signs of holiness, indicators of God's favor, nor proof of a deep prayer life. Teresa of Avila is right on target. We pause and reflect upon her wisdom: 'The highest perfection obviously does not consist in interior delights or in great raptures or in visions or in the spirit of prophecy but in having our will so much in conformity with God's will that there is nothing we know he wills that we do not want with all our desire, and in accepting the bitter as happily as we do the delightful when we know that his majesty desires it.' John of the Cross helps us along as well: 'One act done in charity is more precious in God's sight than all the visions and communications possible... Many individuals who have not received these experiences are incomparably more advanced than others who have received many.'

Indeed, love calls us and challenges us to live in the truth that is the love of Christ. Robert Hugh Benson says it ever so gently in a poem which emphasizes a deepening of the basic beliefs of our faith:

> What hast thou learnt today?
> Hast thou sounded awful mysteries,
> Hast pierced the veiled skies,
> Climbed to the feet of God,
> Trodden where saints have trod,
> Fathomed the heights above?
> Nay,
> This only have I learnt, that God is love.
>
> What hast thou heard today?
> Hast heard the angel trumpets cry,
> And rippling harps reply;
> Heard from the throne of flame
> Whence God incarnate came
> Some thund'rous message roll?
> Nay,
> This have I heard, His voice within my soul.
>
> What hast thou felt today?
> The pinions of the angel guide
> That standeth at thy side
> In rapturous ardours beat,
> Glowing, from head to feet
> In ecstasy divine?
> Nay,
> This only have I felt, Christ's hand in mine.[4]

Soul Afire

Born in 1566, of a noble family in Florence Italy, Mary Magdalene de Pazzi entered the cloistered Carmelite monastery in Florence at age seventeen. Her prayers

and penance were particularly for the reform of the
Church. She suffered much during the last three years
of her life. As her suffering increased, so did her love
for Jesus crucified. Her love was like an inner fire. At
times her inner fire experience of God's love was so
great that it was evident in her actions. She moved
from place to place quickly, and sometimes ran
through the convent crying in a loud voice 'Love, love,
love!' or 'Love is not loved! Love is not loved!' She said
to her sisters 'You do not know, beloved sisters, that
my Jesus is nothing but love, yes, mad with love. You
are mad with love, my Jesus, as I have said and as I
shall always say. You are very lovely and joyous, you
refresh and solace, you nourish and unite. You are both
pain and slaking, toil and rest, life and death in one. Is
there anything that is not within you! You are wise and
willful, lofty and unmeasurable, miraculous and unut-
terable.' She tells us: 'God wants nothing but that the
soul unite with him in such wise, and that he may be
utterly united with her. And when the soul leans her
head against the head of Jesus, she has no other desire
save to unite with God, and to have God unite with
her.' Her understanding of the Church and of herself
as the bride of Christ was complete and total. She told
her sisters: 'In charity we must be cheerful and prompt
knowing that by serving our fellow creatures, we serve
God in his members, and that he regards a service done
to our neighbor as done to himself.'

We all have moments of passion. When they come,
we have a choice for good or ill. A brief look at our
world shows how passions are out of control in
violence of all kinds and at all levels. As Christians we
counteract destructive passions by fervor, devotion
and unflagging interest in causes and activities con-

nected with Christ. Mary Magdalene directed her passion to the love of Christ. We must agree with her that 'Love is not loved' as much as he should be in this world. Jesus who is all love wants our love in return. How do we make this known? It is our duty to show others how to love Jesus and assure them that they are loved by him. The noble call of love is freely offered and freely received. We worship God because he is to be worshiped and through our worship we gratify our deepest and greatest longings.

Our Lord Jesus is like a consuming fire that burns within our souls. When we destroy our evil tendencies, we keep his love in us burning bright. Within our mystic dimension we gaze at the divine flame of love in our souls. When we do this in silence and solitude we know with absolute clarity that these two attributes of Carmel never isolate us or lead us to self absorption. They are essential in making our interior atmosphere receptive to the gentle voice of God. There is a painting of Jesus sitting alone in the desert. The sun is going down and he will be there in prayer throughout the night. Often we are in busy places with lots of people, not unlike Jesus during his three years of active ministry. However, we must follow him to the desert. We can slip away mentally into solitude and silence with Jesus. This solitude is not lonely nor is the silence empty. They are gifts bursting with God, therefore treasures for companionship with God. Solitude and silence are like blinders that keep our spiritual eyes on the flame of God's love. We are blessed by being guided by this living flame. The brighter Jesus' divine flame burns within us, the more beautiful our souls become. We pass on the heat and light from our divine flame by increasing the love we put into our deeds for our family, work, parish, civic and social organizations and other activities in which we are a part.

Living God's Love

The warmth of our prayer and the light from our good works make God easier to find in our society. We must always be open to God's transforming love. It circulates within us so that we can live out holiness as dignified members of God's family. God's love is shown in very simple things: a kind, encouraging, comforting word or phrase, a phone call of support, a letter of love, leaving a situation better than we found it, doing good in small unpretentious ways, not talking above or at another person, or not interrupting him or her. Our quiet light shines when we talk to individuals as fellow human beings. By really listening to, and standing beside them, our presence will encourage them to feel esteem and respect, and be their unique selves.

God's love is also shown in situations that require us to stand up and correct that which is not right. We cannot sit back and let significant inaccuracies pass by. We cannot be indifferent or think that a bad situation will take care of itself. On the other hand, to do for others when they can do for themselves encourages and supports unhealthy dependency. Chronic people-pleasers and others who have marked self defeating defense mechanisms have a way to go before they reach mystical terrain. This land is not for those who have a disordered need for affection, who want to be a member of a spiritually fashionable country club or who desire to live at a top of the line religious resort. If we live the gospel with strength and conviction, we know what we have to do, and we do it. The mountain of God's love is steep and we climb it step by step through growth in self mastery. Life is not a continual pleasure hunt as our society suggests, but continual lessons in learning the art of love. Why is love the hardest virtue in which to grow? Because it requires risk. It takes courage to speak up and make positive gentle corrections. It takes wisdom to avoid rewarding negative behavior. If children are not getting along for a significant period of time we do not give them things to make them stop fighting. We try to uncover the real reason for their fights. If our son has friends or is dating someone who is not right for him, we are not silent. We must directly and firmly voice our intuitions. If we see abuse near at hand, we do not close our eyes to it. We need to take action.

Living God's love and getting along with others is not an option, it is a duty. Peace is worthwhile, even if we have to put up with a little static. Sometimes the truth is hard to hear. Although it may be difficult, objective truth liberates us from confusion and bewilderment. There are occasions when we have private conversations with a loved one. No one is watching us and no one is listening to what is said. During these times, how do we treat our loved ones? How do we treat them as possessions that we mold into our likeness or advantage, or use to fulfill lost dreams? On the other hand, how do we treat them as God's gifts to us that we love, value and appreciate? We cannot be 'completed' by, nor 'find ourselves' in another person. Each of us is unique and we can only find our authentic identity in God. Jesus tells us who we really are; and to this we must listen.

God's love helps us in so many ways. We rarely give up on people of our acquaintance who have bad attitudes. Women are known for pouring out love, especially on their fragile, sinful and blessed family members. People can learn to love little by little, and a sweet smile given for no reason can work wonders. Saying thank you for whatever a person does routinely, is so simple, yet can make all the difference in the world. Our fidelity to prayer leads us to the broken members in our family, parish, workplace and other organizations. In little ways, we try to tend to their painful wounds with love. It is difficult to love people as they are, but we give it our best effort. Prayer leads us to seek counsel from wise persons and gives us the wisdom to see difficult people differently. It softens our hearts. We may have been bothered by people who irritate us, malign us, or do not like us. Now, we put them in the heart of Jesus. When we have frustrations that bring out the worst in us, we put them in Jesus' heart as well. After a few days, we take them out and we are surprised because they are products of new growth for us. Mystic women are never distant from the concerns of life in the world.

Contemplation and action nurture each other. Time spent in contemplative prayer makes us more aware of the suffering and longing of our contemporaries. We have passed through the stages of loving ourselves and loving God for our own sakes. At times we fall back into a 'what's in it for me' mode. However, we pull out of that mentality when we remember how easily the ego edges God out. We also think of the many ways in which we are grateful to God. As we strive to love ourselves and love God for his sake, we become more giving than receiving. We come out of ourselves. If we base our spiritual life on consolations, delights or sweet feelings, we will not get very far. As we wean ourselves from consolations, delights and sweet feelings, we learn to live by faith, faith, faith. In prayer we try to be empty, still and quiet before the majesty of God. As we wait upon him, something unasked for may happen. A thought, or an insight that we never had before, a little grain of understanding, a new way of thinking, a little light shining, a small inspiration to do something more. Something we never noticed before suddenly becomes alive with beauty, awesome wonder happens in a least likely place. Where did it come from? It certainly was not knowledge perceived through our senses. We did not seek it or ask for it. Yet, it is there and brings us closer to God without our direct seeking of it. It was a little nudge from the Holy Spirit, a little mystical gift from God. Such little gifts are precious sweetnesses in the garden of life. Instead of talking to God when we pray, we now listen to him more and allow him to write upon our hearts.

Soul Care

We know that evil wears many disguises and we use precautionary measures to avoid symptoms that could lead to spiritual decay. Armed with a duster and maybe even a brush and cleanser, we remove the cobwebs of evil that nestle and breed in the nooks and crannies of the various rooms in our souls. Negative thoughts abide in those webs. We are still bothered about the friend who was not grateful for the gift we gave her. We are envious of our co-worker who got that promotion we wanted. We haven't received that

call or letter that was promised. We did not get what
we wanted for our birthday. The bank teller gave us a
dark look last week. We feel stress because we hold on
to feelings of divisiveness, revenge, disappointments,
bitterness and indifference. These incidents and many
others are negatives that build upon the negatives in
our past. How often and to what extent is the beauty
of our souls dimmed by our past negatives, our
downbeat internal monologues, our insecurities? How
do we put ourselves down, make the same old excuses
or blame the same people. We cannot change what we
do not define. In order to stop the smoke that darkens
the beauty of our souls, we must stop repeating our
inappropriate defense tactics and clear our minds of
them so we can move ahead. They blind us to what is
good and what is giving within and around us. They
lead to the dysfunctions of feeble soul disease which
weakens our union with God and frays the bonds of
our friendships. We must dust or scrub away these
webs frequently for if we do not, they will grow and
dim, darken and even block the light and beauty of
God's flame of love. If we let these negative, downward spiral thoughts go, Jesus will fill their space and
his flame will burn with new beauty within us.

As we contemplate Jesus' living flame, our allegiance to him, as well as our compassion toward
ourselves and others, will deepen. The peace of Christ
takes the place of our negative thoughts. Our deeds
are reinforced by an interior life that is firm and strong,
and an inner journey that always moves toward Jesus
Christ. A seventeenth-century nun gives us a good
prayer to use as we dust away our cobwebs:

> Lord, you know better than I know myself that
> I am growing older and will someday be old.

Keep me from the fatal habit of thinking I must say something on every subject and on every occasion. Release me from craving to straighten out everybody's affairs. Make me thoughtful, but not moody; helpful, but not bossy. With my vast store of wisdom, it seems a pity not to use it all, but you know Lord that I want a few friends at the end. Keep my mind free from the recital of endless details; give me wings to get to the point. Seal my lips on my aches and pains. They are increasing, and love of rehearsing them is becoming sweeter as the years go by. I dare not ask for grace enough to enjoy the tales of others' pains, but help me to endure them with patience. I dare not ask for improved memory, but for a growing humility and a lessening cocksureness when my memory seems to clash with the memories of others. Teach me the glorious lesson that occasionally I may be mistaken. Keep me reasonably sweet. I do not want to be a saint—some of them are so hard to live with—but a sour old person is one of the crowning works of the devil. Give me the ability to see good things in unexpected places and talents in unexpected people. And, give me, O Lord, the grace to tell them so. Amen.

A mystic's primary responsibility to God, and to the world, is a regular pattern of daily prayer. Prayer is the best food we have to satisfy our hunger for the mysterious God. We pray when we do not taste the sweetness of the Lord, when it is the last thing we want to do, or when our prayers seem useless. Teresa of Avila urges us on:

To persist in prayer without returns, this is not time lost, but a great gain. It is endeavor without thought of self and only for the glory

of the Lord. Even though at first it seems like
the effort is all in vain, it is not so, but it is as
with children who work in their father's fields:
they receive no daily wage but when the year
comes to an end, everything belongs to them.

To know God through prayer supports a life which
seems to be marked by continual changes and continual
adjustments to God's will. God's will calls forth decisions that require the most love from us. As we do God's
will, his tender love will burn in our hearts and flow into
the hearts of the people who are entwined in our lives.
By living prayerfully we image the kind face of Jesus to
humanity. Living prayerfully is not dependent on what
we do. It is dependent on how we live as women of God.
We are always growing and developing as women of
God. Prayer is the foundation that stabilizes and supports our walk with the Lord wherever life leads us.
God's love always transforms. We wake up in the
morning and believe we are going to have a good day.
Goodness is an inside job. Our inner goodness comes
from the goodness of God's presence in our hearts. Our
goodness is sustained and enhanced by the goodness of
Jesus. Our good words and actions are his love made
visible. Through them we build up our personal living
spaces and our society. Mystics are people of hope. That
is why we forgive easily. That is why we believe that
good resides in the deepest depths of people, even the
most hardened. 'That is a good thing!' is such a simple
phrase, but, like a pebble tossed into the water, it makes
positive ripples flow in our pools of life. Hope gives us
the strength to carry on, during good and bad times.
Hope is indispensable and endless.

Today many women in the United States can do
almost anything, anywhere and anytime. We have

more freedom than ever before. Mystics know that a
life devoted to faith and lived in allegiance with Jesus
Christ is the most freeing life of all. The strength of our
faith makes us strong. Like different lanterns, each
with its own shape and size, women mystics reflect
Jesus' light in our sin darkened society, each in her
own way and in her own style. Each lantern is unique
but all have the same flame that burns with the fire of
Jesus' love. We are the caretakers and carriers of that
flame. As we move about with our lanterns, we find
that our flames of love enkindle other flames of love
and thereby lighten up the dark realities of society with
Christ's love. His love lasts forever. By going about
our daily activities in a Christ like way—be it sewing
on a button, doing the shopping, visiting a shut in,
walking while saying the rosary for peace, teaching
catechism, or organizing a parish activity—we become
the change we want to see in our society. As individuals, and by collectively helping each other, it is up to
women to resist and stand firm against abuse and
exploitation, especially of women. Women create and
safeguard the sacredness of life by holding high the
truths of Christ and living out his words. This sustains
life at its highest level and embraces womanhood in
all her beauty. Prayer is our refuge and our strength.
It is a comfort when we experience pain, emptiness,
loneliness, raw emotions or when we feel we cannot
take it anymore. Life is not what we expected it to be.
Life is hard. At times our deepest prayer is a simple
but gut wrenching sigh. Prayer helps us adapt to new
or unforeseen situations and circumstances. When we
learn to let go and really trust in God, we find that
everything can be seen as grace.

One of the times Marguerite Teilhard de Chardin found grace was during the end of her life when she was quite ill. Her prayer was very honest:

> Lord, the day is drawing to a close and, like all the other days, it leaves with me the impression of utter defeat. I have done nothing for you; neither have I said conscious prayers, nor performed works of charity, nor any work at all, work that is sacred for every Christian who understands its significance. I have not even been able to control that childish impatience and those foolish rancours that so often occupy the place that should be yours in the 'no man's land' of my emotions. It is in vain that I promise you to do better. I shall be no different tomorrow, nor on the day that follows.

> When I retrace the course of my life, I am overwhelmed by the same impression of inadequacy. I have sought you in prayer and in the service of my neighbor, for we cannot separate you from our brothers any more than we can separate our body from our spirit. But in seeking you, do I not find myself? Do I not wish to satisfy myself? Those words that I secretly termed good and saintly dissolve in the light of approaching eternity, and I dare no longer lean on these supports that have lost their stability.

> Even actual sufferings bring me no joy, because I bear them so badly. Perhaps we are all like this: incapable of discerning anything but our own wretchedness and our own despairing cowardice before the light of the Beyond that waxes on our horizon.

> But it may be, O Lord, that this impression of privation is part of a divine plan. It maybe that,

in your eyes, self complacency is the most obnoxious of all fripperies, and that we must come before you naked so that you, you alone, may clothe us.

Absolute Trust

Marguerite's words give life to Catherine of Siena's phrase: 'Lose yourself wholly; and the more you lose, the more you will find.' There are many times in our lives when the only thing we can do is throw ourselves in the ocean of God's love. Indeed, we must leave our past to God's mercy, our present to his trust and our future to his goodness. We know not what lies ahead for us. How does sickness show us who we are and help us discover who we can be? If the time should come when we are bed bound and unable to do anything we can still love God. When Jesus was on the cross he said 'My God, my God why have you forsaken me.' His words were an expression of his utter human desolation. He felt and experienced the deepest pain of being abandoned by humanity and by God. These are the words of the first line of Psalm 22. Many times we feel like crying out these words of Jesus.

However, when reinforced by grace, we think of places where God is abandoned, ignored, forgotten, not cared about and to all these places we send prayers of love, adoration, atonement and reparation. We are agents through which a loving homage to God becomes present in these places. We give our suffering to God our Father as an act of love for the entire world. Suffering through no fault of our own is a strong witness. A vibrant soul can thrive in a frail body. Pain can be a motivator of change toward the good and toward God. Unencumbered by projects, ambitions, grand plans or other great distractions, we who suffer become channels of the love of Jesus crucified. Broken by pain we unite ourselves to Jesus on the cross and send our love to the broken people and broken places in the human family. Pain and love connect us all. Prayers from a hospital bed are stronger than we can imagine. God chooses the weak to confound the strong. If we look intensely, we find an indescribable, deep, and mysterious beauty that does not fade in Christians who are fragile, infirm or old. Jesus suffers in those who suffer and he uses their pain for the redemption of humanity.

In Watertown, New York there is a monastery of contemplative, cloistered nuns who are dedicated to the adoration of the precious blood of Jesus Christ. Some time ago, the nuns printed the following poem on a card. The author is unknown.

> God sends his heaviest crosses
> To those he calls his own,
> And the bitterest drops of the chalice
> Are reserved for his friends alone.

> But the blood red drops are precious,
> And the crosses are all gain,
> For joy is bought with sacrifice,
> And the price of love is pain.

A mystic orientation does not remove us from the concerns of the world, but brings a spirit of prayer, hope, faith and the presence of God to the concerns of the human condition. The mystic finds God's presence in the very ordinary: a bouquet of flowers sitting on a counter, clouds in the sky, a child learning to read, old folks playing bingo. There are unknown, hidden, God related meanings in the commonplace. So many times, there are deeper meanings than that which is obvious.

John Paul II said 'In the designs of Providence, there are no mere coincidences.'[5] And so it is true.

As mystics we believe that true compassion begins by holding others in prayer. Compassionate prayer bears fruit in humanity through the use of our gifts and talents, and in ways unknown to us. Mystics do not have a 'me and Jesus' mentality, but rather a 'me, Jesus and the human family' outlook. A mystical orientation gives us strength to be God's lowly servants. As his servants our service will not be tainted by the self seeking endeavors that can occur in the administration and provision of services. We mature in the spirit of service, rather than use the service as an escape, egocentric need fulfillment, obsession, or the primary description of our identity. The mystic is always vigilant so that good intentions or good activities do not become exalted beyond their value or an end in themselves. If they are carried to extremes, good things can become distorted.

Our works of service are channels by which we are transformed. We strive to be better than we used to be. We cannot quench our thirst for God with anything finite. God resides at the center of our souls and we must not let good people, good causes, cultural icons, charismatic leaders, possessions, projects, persons that speak of God, our personal experiences of God or our personal experiences of prayer take the place of God at our center. They may help us on the road to God, but are not a replacement for the mysterious God within us. Ah, and he is such a mystery. We are surrounded by mystery, which cannot be understood by our human minds. The more we study and meditate on Jesus, the more mysterious he becomes. Our Catholic religion is replete with mystery: The Trinity, the

Eucharist, the sacraments and the Holy Sacrifice of the Mass. Mystery is unfathomable; there is no bottom line, no end of the road, no finished masterwork. Inscrutable and impenetrable, at best we know its wisdom from shadows.

Each mystic is unique; there are no two alike. However, the mystics' common connection is to seek and love God, to renew and strengthen the world through the teachings of Christ and to be comfortable with mystery. We can be called stewards of mystery. We are immersed in it, not so much to find answers to our questions, but to rest in, and be transformed by, the questions themselves. The entire world is held together in the mystery of Christ. Augustine sheds some light on the shadows of mystery: 'What you do not understand, treat with reverence and be patient; and what you do understand, cherish and keep.'[6]

What are some guidelines that indicate we have a healthy mystical orientation? Max Ehrmann assists us:

Go placidly amid the noise and haste,
and remember what peace there may be in silence.
As far as possible without surrender
be on good terms with all persons.
Speak your truth quietly and clearly;
and listen to others,
even the dull and the ignorant;
they too have their story.

Avoid loud and aggressive persons,
they are vexations to the spirit.
If you compare yourself with others,
you may become vain and bitter;
for always there will be greater and lesser persons than yourself.
Enjoy your achievements as well as your plans.

Keep interested in your own career, however humble;
it is a real possession in the changing fortunes of time.
Exercise caution in your business affairs;
for the world is full of trickery.
But let this not blind you to what virtue there is;
many persons strive for high ideals;
and everywhere life is full of heroism.

Be yourself.
Especially, do not feign affection.
Neither be cynical about love;
for in the face of all aridity and disenchantment
it is as perennial as the grass.

Take kindly the counsel of the years,
gracefully surrendering the things of youth.
Nurture strength of spirit to shield you in sudden
misfortune.
But do not distress yourself with dark imaginings.
Many fears are born of fatigue and loneliness.
Beyond a wholesome discipline,
be gentle with yourself.

You are a child of the universe,
no less than the trees and the stars;
you have a right to be here.
And whether or not it is clear to you,
no doubt the universe is unfolding as it should.

Therefore be at peace with God,
whatever you conceive Him to be,
and whatever your labors and aspirations,
in the noisy confusion of life keep peace with your soul.

With all its sham, drudgery, and broken dreams,
it is still a beautiful world.
Be cheerful.
Strive to be happy.[7]

Jesus Christ is the source of our true happiness. His heart
is where we rest and abide. In the stillness of sacred

moments, the eyes of our soul gaze upon Jesus. We see
his ever changing and infinitely radiant beauty. We are
lifted up and captivated by this beauty. We listen, in
receptive silence, to what he tells us. We can only listen
with the ears of our soul. Anything we say or think will
mar his intense beauty and what he is telling us. If we
had a shred of understanding of Jesus' love for us, we
would be stunned into daily reform. Yes, we listen and
listen, and then we do whatever he tells us.

John of the Cross wrote *The Spiritual Canticle*. It
remains to this day, a spiritual masterpiece of loving
exchanges between the soul and her most beloved
bridegroom Jesus. The stanzas are intimate conversations between them. In his prologue John states that
the stanzas are love's utterances that arise from deep
mystical wisdom. He explains God's intense communication with the soul. 'It should be known that this
touch of a spark is a very subtle touch which the
beloved sometimes produces in the soul even when
least expected, and which inflames her in the fire of
love, as if a hot spark were to leap from the fire and
set her ablaze. Then with remarkable speed, as when
one suddenly remembers, the will is enkindled in
loving, desiring, praising and thanking God and
reverencing, esteeming and praying to him in savor of
love. She calls these acts flowing from the balsam of
God.' John of the Cross illustrates how, once Jesus is
truly known and loved as a bridegroom, ones life
changes. The soul's love for her spouse Jesus is very,
very deep. It fills the heart to capacity and overflows
into the lives of others. Our love for God, for ourselves,
for others and for our occupations are properly
ordered, and tended to in such a way that sanctifies

everyone we know and everything we do. John of the Cross illustrates how this is done:

> My beloved is my bridegroom
> And my Lord—O what a joy!
> I will henceforth all the powers
> Of my soul for him employ;
> and the flock that once I tended,
> Now I tend not as before
> For my only occupation
> Is to love him more and more.
>
> I have gone away forever
> From the haunts of idle men
> And a sharer in their follies
> I will never be again.
> They may say, and say it loudly;
> I am lost, but I am not;
> I was found by my beloved
> O how blessed is my lot.[8]

Notes

1   Pope Benedict XVI, *Homily for the beginning of his Petrine Ministry* (24 April 2005).

2   Congregation for Institutes of Consecrated Life and for Societies of Apostolic Life, Instruction on the Contemplative Life and on the Enclosure of Nuns *Verbi Sponsa* , 4.

3   Pope Benedict XVI, Post-synodal Apostolic Exhortation *Verbum Domini*.

4   R. H. Benson, 'After a Retreat'.

5   Pope John Paul II, *Discourse in the Chapel of the Apparitions at Fatima* (12 May 1982).

6   St Augustine, *Sermon 51*, 35.

7   Max Ehrmann, *Desiderata* (1952).

8   A paraphrase of some verses from the *Spiritual Canticle* of St John of the Cross.

10

BLESS THIS HOME LORD,
AND FILL IT WITH YOUR LOVE

mystic woman's road of life has its share of hills and valleys, ups and downs. No one is immune from discouraging times. Once, when Teresa of Avila was riding in a covered wagon to found a new Carmel, the wagon overturned while crossing a river. Teresa was thrown into the water. She was dripping wet and discouraged. She complained to the Lord and then heard the words: 'Teresa, this is how I treat my friends.' Her response was immediate: 'Well, that is why you have so few!' Teresa's direct sense of humor helped her to cope with many disappointments. They are a common part of life. Our Lord Jesus experienced disappointments. A great disappointment occurred when he was in the Garden of Gethsemane. With his customary candor, Jesus asked his apostles who were asleep during his agony in the garden: 'Can't you even spend one hour with me?'

We work hard on a dinner and receive no compliments from our guests. We just finished cleaning our home. It is spotless and in come our kids with their dirt. We made our husband's favorite dessert and he did not even notice it. A friend we thought we could rely on turns away. The things we hoped would happen did

not happen. Our sister deeply loved her fiance and was
rejected a week before their wedding. A mother with
three children is suddenly stricken with cancer. There
are innumerable examples of disappointments in life.
Everyone has them. Ella Wheeler Wilcox once penned:

> It is easy enough to be pleasant,
>   when life flows by like a song,
> But the man worthwhile is one who will smile,
>   when everything goes dead wrong.
> For the test of the heart is trouble,
>   and it always comes with the years.
> And the smile that is worth the praises of earth,
>   is the smile that shines through the tears.[1]

Sometimes disappointments are the shadow of God's
protective wings. The event that caused the disappointment may not have been good for us or for our
souls. God knew things about the situation that we did
not know. In disappointment and suffering we can
find a call by God to an intimacy with him that would
otherwise be lost to us. A man, brilliant and financially
successful, became the father of a retarded daughter.
He wondered why, but later discovered that if he had
not had that child he would have lost his soul to the
goods and gods of worldly success. She taught him
what love is. Within a family, having a child who has
a serious disorder or disability, or who is gifted, is a
challenge and a gift. Out of the ordinary circumstances
can set him or her apart. Circumstances can be used to
get love and other things, cause undue dependence or
inappropriate behavior, or be the source of other out
of the ordinary problems. For these and other reasons,
it is good to be connected with a few people who have
accurate knowledge of the disorder, disability or gift.
Competent people can be resources for encourage-

ment, support, helpful suggestions and coping skills related to the special need.

Here is a story that shows how a terminal illness can change one's orientation and bring one closer to God; it is an excerpt from *Testament of Friendship* by Vera Brittain:

> On one of the coldest mornings of that spring, after she had learned from a London specialist that she might not have more than two years to live, she went for a walk past Clare Leighton's cottage to a farm further up the hill. She felt tired and dejected; her mind, still vigorously alive in her slow, impaired body, rebelled bitterly against her fate. Why, she wondered, should she, at 33, not yet in the fullness of her developing powers, be singled out for this cruel unforeseen blow? She knew, for the constant demands of her friends had made it clear to her, that her life was infinitely valuable to others. She thought of all the half dead people who could put in time as though time were not the greatest gift in the universe, while she, who could use it so superbly was soon to be deprived of it for ever, and she felt that her mind could hardly contain the rising anguish of that realization.
>
> Just then she found herself standing by a trough outside the farmyard, the water in it was frozen and a number of young lambs were struggling beside it vainly trying to drink. She broke the ice for them with her stick, and as she did so she heard a voice within her saying 'Having nothing, yet possessing all things.' It was so distinct that she looked round, startled, but she was alone with the lambs on the top of the hill. Suddenly in a flash, the grief, the bitterness, the sense of frustration disappeared; all desire to

possess power and glory for herself vanished away, and never came back. She walked down the hill with the exhilaration which, says Storm Jameson in *Civil Journey*, 'springs from the sense of having lost everything. It is a feeling like no other, a curious form of spiritual intoxication, perhaps not repeatable.'

Winifred never told me of this incident nor of the sentence of death passed upon her, until June 1935 when she had only three months to live. By that time she thought, or as I now suspect, allowed me to believe that she thought, that she had outwitted the doctors. The moment of 'conversion' on the hill at Monks Risborough, she said with tears in her eyes, was the supreme spiritual experience of her life.

Yes, sometimes discouraging moments become defining moments. They change the course of our lives. Personal tragedy can be a movement of grace that redefines our existence. Other less dramatic incidents can be defining moments as well. Edith Stein discovered and read the autobiography of Teresa of Avila in one night while visiting a friend. After finishing it she exclaimed 'This is truth.' and changed her life's direction by embracing the Catholic faith. Defining moments in our lives are shaped by faith and love. God reveals to us divine secrets within our defining moments. John of the Cross wrote:

> Seek him in faith and love, without desiring to find satisfaction in anything other than what you ought to know. Faith and love are like the blind person's guides. They will lead you along a path unknown to you, to the place where God is hidden. Faith... is comparable to the feet by which one journeys to God, and love is like one's

guide. In dealing with these mysteries and secrets of faith, the soul will merit through love the discovery of the content of faith, that is the bridegroom whom she desires to possess in this life through the special grace of divine union with God... and in the next life through the essential glory, by which she will rejoice in him not in a hidden way, but 'face to face' (1 Cor 13:12).

Anchored in Hope

The road to holiness is open to everyone. We go forward on the wheels of conversion. We move ahead in fits and starts, with a steadfast gaze on Jesus. Conversion happens, often without us noticing it. When our eyes drift to narcissistic desires, we slide backward into the mud of egocentricities. Mystic women can still whine, whimper or use other ways to feel sorry for ourselves. However, we know the dangers of continually acting like scared little girls who always apologize, cower in weakness, turn their geese into swans, do not see things as they are or do not stand up for themselves. Exhibiting these behaviors in order to avoid getting hurt does not work. There is no safe refuge from problems. They are a normal part of life. With God's help, we acknowledge and define our fears and other related negative experiences connected with our concerns. What are they and where do they come from? We work with them under the lights of faith and hope. When we understand them better, we can move ahead.

It takes courage to stop looking back, to forgive ourselves and to discontinue repetitive negative mind tapes. We take steps forward by descending into the quiet of our souls. Here we find that although the problems and frustrations of women have common areas, they are mostly individual because of individual weaknesses. Common solutions to problems and frustrations are rare due to the varying levels of common sense, motivation, determination, perseverance and daily prayer present in each woman. A solution for one person does not necessarily work for another. In the quiet of our souls we face, ask and answer the hard questions within each of our lives. We do this within the context of seeing our individual lives as unique, valuable and blessed gifts from God.

Then we begin anew. We see the good that comes from acknowledging and expressing our disappointments and fears; they become a positive warning system that alerts us to action and change. Our pain is real; however, it may not be as debilitating as we once thought. With that knowledge we release it. When downward spiral thoughts associated with our pain are released, courage and strength are re established, and supported by hope. Hope is not wishful thinking or unfounded expectations. It reinforces the prospect of new growth and imbues individuals with courage in trying situations. Hope anticipates positive aspects about what an individual is becoming. It is so needed when taking risks that go beyond comfort zones, with no guarantee as to where it will all end. Acceptance of our trials leads us to new insights. The worst disappointments can become great graces.

Our personal share of suffering is never useless. It is an effective tool for the good of our families and others because it is inseparable from Jesus' redeeming love. Hope is like a little bird who sweetly sings in the darkest part of the night. She knows the dawn will come. In the midst of our disappointments, we do not feel inclined to sing, but our little chirps verify our belief in hope. Hope does not let discouragement become deep or lasting or get the best of us. Indeed, hope is our greatest strength when all seems doomed to failure. It draws out our inner beauty and the rest of the best in us. Because discouragement easily results from disappointment, it is best to face discouragement head on. Pray about it, talk about it to significant others and eventually it will be resolved. In the great lawn of life the weeds of discouragement are usually easily pulled out. The confusion of a pile of weeds is calmed by the green of the everlasting hills.

Hope is not the same as optimism or positive thinking. It is much more. Hope fastens everything on the truth that in and through our deepest and most profound suffering and emptiness, God is somehow mysteriously present. We cannot say or think how this is so. We only know that hope gives life. We hold on to the high aspirations of our Christian life despite the futility and fragmentation of society around us. We find wholeness in the teachings and traditions of our Church and know that chaos can be turned into order by the cross of Christ. God's will is a gradual plan that unfolds all through our lives. He speaks to us through desolation and setbacks. And many times he surprises us with good things of which we never even dreamed. Teresa of Avila puts things in their proper order: 'Let your desire be to see God; your fear to lose him, your grief to be separated from him, your joy in whatsoever may take you to him; thus you will live in profound peace.'

Blessings Abound

An apron has long been used to protect clothing from spills and splatters. In days of yore, when religious habits were more common then they are now, a part of the habit was called a scapular. It represented the yoke of Christ, consisted of two panels of cloth joined across the shoulders and covered the back and front of the full length habit. The word scapular comes from the Latin *scapula* which is also the name of the two large flat triangular bones of the shoulder. Originally the scapular was worn to protect the tunic, the long gown that was the major part of the habit, from dirt and stain. It was an apron. Sometimes in biblical pictures we can see a man wearing a scapular style apron.

There are about eighteen scapulars that have Church approval. These days, they are usually two small pieces of cloth joined by strings and worn around the neck and underneath clothing. They usually symbolize an association with, or attachment to, a religious order within the Church. The best known scapulars are: white (the Holy Trinity) red (the passion of Christ) black (the seven sorrows of Mary) blue (the Immaculate Conception) and brown (Our Lady of Mount Carmel).

The scapular is a symbol of the yoke of Christ. We are joined with Jesus and work together with him. Jesus is the incarnation of God the Father's love for us. Jesus founded the Church as a continual sign of his love for us, and as the way that would lead us to the Father. Jesus gave us his mother, Mary. She is our mother and shows us how to live in faith. We need signs and symbols to express relationships, to mark the passage of time, to indicate deep realities, and to remind us of who we are and where we are headed. Symbol comes from a Greek word that means to bring together.

The brown scapular is the most common of all the scapulars. It is an external symbol of Mary's love for us, of the trust we have in her, and of our commitment to live like her. The brown scapular symbolizes a way of life especially dedicated to Mary. How is this expressed? We trust in her protection and aspire to be like her in her commitment to Christ and to others. We look to Mary to teach us how to be open to God, and how to do what he wants us to do in the circumstances of our lives. We are Mary's students. She teaches us to listen to the word of God in the bible and in life, and to believe in God's word by putting it into practice. Mary's scapular is a reminder to pray every day and to look for the presence of God in everything that happens to us. The Mother of God shows us how to be involved with people in a loving, attentive and caring way. The brown scapular is not a magical cloth that will bring us good fortune or a lucky charm to keep us from harm. It is not a key that will automatically open the gates of heaven, a guarantee of salvation, or something we use as an excuse for not living up to the demands of Christian life. The brown scapular is a constant reminder of our commitment, which began at baptism when we became children of God, to follow Jesus as Mary did. The brown scapular motivates us to keep climbing up the rugged spiritual slopes of Mount Carmel, and validates our belief that when we reach the end of our trail on earth, we will see God in the everlasting hills of heaven.

Catholics were usually enrolled in the brown scapular a few days before they made their first communion. Enrollment by a priest, or other authorized person, is only needed once. A brown scapular can be replaced by a scapular medal. The brown scapular is a sacramental that constantly reminds us to live authentic Christian lives by reflecting teachings of the gospel, receiving the sacraments, having a special devotion to Mary, being kind to everyone and belonging to the family of Carmel. Wearing the brown scapular is a sign that we live in the company of Mary.

Our beloved and 'be not afraid' Pope John Paul II said he was formally enrolled in the brown scapular as a child and he wore it until his death. He had a great affection for the Carmelite order. He reflected the spirituality of Carmel by being a contemplative in an active world and living each day in the presence of God. The title of his doctoral thesis was *The Doctrine of Faith According to St John of the Cross*. The thesis showed his love and esteem for John of the Cross, and emphasized the personal nature of an individual's meeting with God—which is the center of every Christian's life. John Paul II said the call of Carmel was 'to be an oasis of contemplation and spirituality where people of the twenty-first century can receive authentic spiritual values.'[2]

We are not mystics just because we put on a scapular. Mysticism is not something we gain by wearing certain clothing, something we earn through academic pursuits, nor something we work toward by esthetical practices. Neither is it an aim, goal, or something we achieve or express through our devotion to God. We are aware of our mystic dimension to the degree that we know how to 'be' in God's love. The way we prepare ourselves to 'be' is by offering ourselves to God and waiting. We are patient, open and receptive to what he gives to us.

Most of all we are always learning to be true disciples of Jesus. He is the summit of our loyalty, allegiance and love. Karl Rahner once said: 'The

Christian of the future will be a mystic or will not be a Christian at all.'[3] A simple yet profound definition of mystic is one who is an intimate friend of Jesus Christ. Mysticism is the full flowering of the grace one has received at baptism. The way we live in the love of Jesus is measured by the way we treat others, and ourselves. We reflect on the beauty of Therese's words 'In the heart of the Church, my mother, I shall be love.' To be love is the woman mystic's quiet energizer. Love takes us to God and takes us to our brothers and sisters. Love comes from the heart and goes to the heart. By giving tender love, women have the privilege of being love at the heart of the Church.

Through love, the mystic woman continues to make God's tenderness known on the earth. Therese of Lisieux said: 'One is consumed by love only in the measure that one surrenders oneself to love.' The ties that bind are frequently the ties that physically, psychologically and spiritually nourish others. The love we have for those in our home and other special people, overflow and enhance the love we show toward our acquaintances, associates and others. The more we learn to love, which is a life long adventure, the more we learn to listen and see with the heart. We give through our own uniqueness and creative abilities. Because we believe in heaven, we realize that what we have, we cannot keep, and what we give away we keep forever. The more we give, the more we realize that we are all partners and companions on the face of this earth. When we build up our own families, we build up the family of God.

Our ability to love depends on our friendship with Jesus. We must always be open to him. The awareness of and growth in the mystical dimension is pure gift from God. Each person has a unique and beautiful mystical dimension even if he or she does not recognize it, or understand it. Sometimes this dimension is manifest in the 'ah' moments of life. More often, the manifestations are best left unspoken, unexplained and even without thought. Shrouded in mysterious graces, they give glory to God in little ways, and sometimes they are only recognized by our souls. Mystic moments can happen anywhere and mystics can be found everywhere. There are more mystics outside monastery walls than inside the cloisters. Many mystics find their path to God between the stove and the kitchen sink. Our Church has often been referred to as a mother and teacher of all nations. As women of today's Church we are mothers and teachers within our homes and surrounding environments within these nations. And the most important thing we can do as mothers and teachers is to pray for our family.

Lord, please bless my children. Protect them by day and night. Lead them down the right roads, forever in thy sight.

Let them know thy presence each step along the way. Giving strength and courage to sustain them, come what may.

Be their consolation in times of woe and strife. Guide them past the pitfalls on their journey through this life.

And when this life is over, see them safely to that shore, where peace and love are boundless, beyond Heaven's golden door.[4]

If we sit still, in the quiet of our kitchens, many good thoughts come to mind. We ponder the words of Brother Lawrence of the Resurrection who entered the Discalced Carmelites in Paris. He had no desire to be a cook when he became a lay brother there, but served the large community in that capacity for fifteen years. This service became his school of sanctity. He wrote:

> I possess God as tranquilly in the bustle of my kitchen... as if I were on my knees before the Blessed Sacrament... It is not necessary to have great things to do. I turn my little omelet in the pan for the love of God. . . When I cannot do anything else, it is enough for me to have lifted a straw from the earth for the love of God.

We realize how many gifts come and go from this most giving room of our home. We find more creative love flowing from the kitchen than from any other room in the house. Food and family are connected in several ways. Certain foods, customs, and small daily rituals at meals bond family members with each other. We receive countless gifts from God, and from our kitchen we give countless gifts to others. Every meal we prepare for our loved ones is a gift, even if we do not feel the giftedness at the time. All good things are meant to be shared. We are very grateful to God for his gifts and respond to God's blessings by preparing and serving meals to others. Meals and food gifts can be benedictions—blessings from our home.

Prayer is a great blessing in more ways than we realize. We pray for all who work in the food industry, we have cooking prayers and thanksgiving prayers after meals. Prayer leads us to action because action is the fruit of prayer. When the common acts of our regular life become more thoughtful and more tender with positive love, they lead us back to contemplating Christ in prayer. As we learn more about God through prayer, others learn more about God through our good conduct. When we are motivated by God's love, we become more loving toward the people and the situations in our lives. We show our gratitude for the bounty of God. We feed each other in many ways. We make wise choices from the cornucopias of fruits and vegetables available for our use. Careful selection of the food we eat, good meal preparation skills, and minimum waste are signs of ecological responsibility. We eat moderately so that others may eat. Mutual sharing, support, encouragement, and peaceful conversations bring unity to the home. Dining with good manners, courteous and respectful behavior, and pleasant uplifting conversation, with light classical music turns a routine meal into a charming dining experience. A calm, leisurely meal makes us aware of the unseen guest at our table—Jesus. He is found in the hearts of the loved ones around us. Issues that cause tension or heated arguments are not for mealtime. Instead, we can show our appreciation of others, not only to family members who prepare the food, but also to the farmers, pickers, packers, transporters and sellers. We are grateful for their work.

The Mystery of Sacrifice

There was an American soldier in France when World War II ended. The young soldier came upon a Catholic church in a small French town. There was a statue of Jesus lying on the ground. He picked it up and saw that it was intact, except for one thing: The hands of Jesus were smashed away. The soldier took some paper from his bag, wrote a message and placed the paper at the base of the statue. The message he wrote was: 'I have no hands but yours.'

Jesus is our greatest example of sacrificial love. He showed his love by giving something of himself to each person he met. When he was giving to others, he must have had mothers in mind. He knew they would carry out his teachings by their lives of sacrifice. Sacrifice is the language of love. Parents live for the good of their children. They make many sacrifices in order to feed, clothe, educate and shelter their children. Their personal dreams are usually put on hold for the sake of raising their family. A mother's life is not her own. Preparing meals and other repetitive tasks within the home can become a rather dull duty with no apparent rewards. Yet, under the duty there is love. No task is too small or too insignificant if it is done with love. Ordinary tasks done with love become extraordinary gifts. Parents are the hands of Christ as they care for their children and other family members. Mostly everything they do for them is based on love. It is not idealized love, but rather love that is found in the trenches.

Those whom we deeply care about have the power to hurt us the most because we love them the most. Archbishop Alban Goodier sums up love in this way:

> When you first pursue love it will be beautiful and rewarding and you will run on. But then it will become painful and demanding. It will see you give all of your strength and have nothing left and ask for more. It will see you laying broken and bleeding by the side of the road and it will pass you by. It will demand of you and reproach you when you haven't more to give. And if you persevere, and if you see love all the way out to the finish, if then there is nothing left, then you will come by reason of love, to what the eye has not seen, or ear has not heard, and it has not even entered into the hearts of men to think those things that God has prepared for those who love him.

John Paul II expressed his gratitude to women: 'Thank you, every woman, for the simple fact of being a woman. Through the insight which is so much a part of your womanhood, you enrich the world's understanding and help to make human relations more honest and authentic.'[5] He continues:

> For in giving themselves to others each day, women fulfill their deepest vocation. Perhaps more than men, women acknowledge the person, because they see persons with their hearts. They see them independently of various ideological or political systems. They see others in their greatness and limitations; they try to go out to them and help them.[6]

Yes, we truly appreciate the women who strive to better themselves and those around them.

Transformation

It usually takes a long time, but at some point we let go of our own ideas about God, concepts of holiness, definitions of love, and let God form us in his image. This resembles being a ball of yarn that is unwound. We let God form us in the way he wants. He is knitting us into something new. Yes, it is the same yarn, but we are formed into something better than ever before. We do not even get to pick the colors or the pattern. Our deep longing for the Lord urges us forward into the unknown. Whatever we understood about God is replaced by a profound sense of mystery. His mystery is present and reverenced. There are sacramentals, signposts pointing toward God, everywhere. The lilies of the fields, clouds, fall foliage, migrating birds, the turning of the seasons, watching seeds become flowers, the shade of the trees and most of all the wonder of birth all open us up to the mystery and majesty of God. Scientific explanations cannot take the mystery out of life. Everything is transformed. We are changing as we are knit into a new pattern. This takes much courage because it is frightening. It can also increase our strength and allow us to recapture innocence. Let us learn of the goodness in change through this little story by an unknown author:

> A stream was moving across the country, experiencing little difficulty. It ran around rocks and through mountains. Then it arrived at a desert. Just as it had crossed every other barrier, the stream tried to cross this one, but it found that as fast as it ran into the sand, its waters disappeared. After many attempts it appeared that there was no way it could continue the journey. Then a voice came in the wind, 'If you stay the way you are, you cannot cross the sands. To go further, you will have to lose yourself.' 'But if I lose myself,' the stream cried, 'I will never know what I'm suppose to do.' 'Oh, on the contrary,' said the voice, 'If you lose yourself, you will become more than you ever dreamed you could be.' So the stream surrendered to the drying sun. And the clouds into which it was formed were carried by the raging wind for many miles. Once it crossed the desert, the stream poured down from the skies, fresh and clean, and full of the energy that comes from storms.

We are reminded of the words of Jesus here: 'Unless a grain of wheat falls to the ground and dies, it remains just a grain of wheat; but if it dies, it produces much fruit' (John 12:24).

By being more in harmony with the mysteries in our lives and in tune with our contemplative nature, we learn to work in a contemplative manner. Since our time of prayer is manifest by a prayerful presence outside of prayer, we are able to attend to the task at hand. There is a peaceful concentration on the various aspects of the task. When we mop the floor we are mindful of our immediate surroundings but purposefully follow a methodical course of action. We rarely think about what else needs to be done, or have significant distractions. Nor would we be startled if we were interrupted. Watching the way a person mops the floor in a contemplative way would be more illuminating than a talk on meditation.

Our work is an expression of our love for God. The contemplative dimension is evident through the mopping experience rather than through ideas about contemplative mopping. The way a person mops exudes peace. One does not attack the dirt on the floor as one so often crumples a piece of paper before it is thrown away. The mop is moved with a gentleness that has a tranquil influence. There is, at that moment, no better use of one's time. One savors the present moment but does not dawdle. Indeed we have the brush and the colors to paint the environment in which we live. We can create peace and light or discord and dark. The way we do our work reverberates into our home, somewhat like the sound of a chime vibrates through a room. With our words and actions we do our best to harmonize and unify our family.

It no longer matters if our prayer is difficult. Prayer can be laborious like rowing a rowboat. Rowing requires work, strength and endurance. After all that effort, we find we only have moved a short distance. Prayer can also be sweet. There is no labor because it is as if we are drifting in a sailboat. We sit back, relax, let God fill our sails and off we go for a long distance in a short time. Teresa of Avila reminds us that we never stand still on our spiritual road. We are either moving forward or moving backward. Prayer gives us courage to face and live the truths of our faith, and of our lives, which make us whole and strong. The depths of our work a day prayer is reflected in the depths of our holiness in life. As we deepen our communion with God, we become stronger in the Christian attributes of our lives. God is the meaning, source and center of life. A life blessed with profound prayer is a life graced by indescribable beauty.

In the Carmelite tradition, contemplative prayer is always a gift from God to us. Contemplative prayer usually does not last long. Contemplative prayer may sound lofty. However, it is commonplace among Christians, though uniquely experienced by each Christian. Often subtle and delicate, it can easily be missed by us. It is closer to air from the movement of a butterfly's wings than wind from the wings of an eagle. Contemplative prayer can be a bewilderment. Why is this so? When we receive this gift, why can't we define or describe it?

Simply put, contemplative prayer is beyond our comprehension. Nothing we do can start, stop, shorten or lengthen it. It cannot be perceived through our senses, nor is it repeatable, measurable or something we can prove. We cannot follow a set of instructions, techniques or methods to receive this gift. Neither can it be explained by intellectual concepts, images or ideas. At best, our attempts to talk about contemplative prayer are limited to word sketches.

Contemplative prayer appears as a loving, gentle immersion in God. We seem captivated or absorbed by him. We rest in the wonder of prayer. We are still and calm, wordless in awe and adoration at the One who loves us. To be spiritually content with 'being' in our Beloved, is to be utterly serene and simple. Afterward, we experience a continuous, peaceful joy at our deepest center, but we cannot put it into words. Following contemplative prayer, we see more beauty in creation because we have a greater appreciation of the Creator. We have a greater awareness of God, but this does not interfere with what we do. Rather, it helps us do things better. Our daily trials are no longer a worrisome concern because we see them in the long view of life. We radiate holiness when we do what Jesus would do in our situations. Holiness is grasped and lived when selfish tendencies are identified and relinquished.

In order to seek the splendor of the Lord we must shun the distractions of this world. We pray for our brothers and sisters whose first concern is pleasure and profit, often at the expense of others. Their last concern is to get into heaven, with as little effort as possible. There are no cheap tickets to heaven. A mystic's first concern is the care of the soul. When soul care has first priority, care of the body and mind falls into place.

We welcome Jesus to be with us in whatever we do, from decorating a cake to driving a tractor. Jesus is with us. He loves us and cares for us. He is content with our work, play, study, entertainment, friends, social groups and worship activities. Holiness thrives when our most beloved companion is by our side. Jesus helps us beyond description when we answer the call to holiness, which is rooted in a deep prayer life, a contemplative presence and union with the

Triune God. This is the call of every Christian, and it is up to us to respond to it every day of our lives.

Mystic moments are also commonplace. They are segments of time that glow with the sacred. They are moments outside of regular time as we know it, where we are seemingly lifted above the daily humdrum of life. We feel drawn up into the awesome, quiet, sustaining reality that God is the most real and the best good; and that what he created is good and beautiful. The gift of human life is the most precious of God's created gifts, and we can only stand mute in wonder at the love God has for each one of us. Indeed, life is full of mystical surprises. Let us look at the best of surprises, which are blessings. Through them we can see how our lives are tapestries of blessings. The anonymous author of these blessings gives us much to ponder:

> May the God of compassion be with us, holding us close when we are weary and hurt and alone, when there is rain in our hearts; and may we be the warm hands and the warm eyes of compassion for people when they reach out to us in need; may the blessings of compassion be on us.

> May the God of peace be with us, ever drawing us into the tabernacle of our hearts; where burns his inner, silent circle of light; may the flame of love kindled by his love ignite in us the gift of being a resting place where the weary world can place its burden; may the blessing of peace be on us.

> May the God of gentleness be with us, caressing us with sunlight and rain and wind; may his tenderness shine through us to warm all who are hurt and lonely; may the blessing of gentleness be on us.

May the God of simplicity touch us with a touch
that empties us, and move us with a simplicity
that simplifies us, so that with clear vision we
may sink into the center of our own poverty
and feel the doors fly open into infinite
freedom, into a wealth which is perfect because
none of it is ours and yet it all belongs to us;
may the blessing of simplicity be on us.

May the God of joy echo in the caverns of our
being, sing its song in our hearts, lift us up and
carry us above all pleasures, because we are not
created for pleasure only, but for joy; may the
song we sing awaken the song that sleeps at the
heart of all we touch, and may the blessing of
joy be on us.

May the God of patience be with us, waiting for
us with outstretched arms, letting us find out
for ourselves; and may our patience with all the
young who fall from small heights and the old
who fall from greater heights be our patience,
and may the blessing of patience be on us.

May the God of love be with us, immersing us in
the rivers of tranquility that flow from him into
the whole universe and draw all things back into
him; may he well up through the dark depths of
our emptiness and frailty, into life giving springs,
flowing through his creation, restoring and filling
all things with life and goodness and strength,
may the blessing of love be on us.

May the God of mercy be with us, forgiving us,
beckoning us, encouraging us to say: 'Now I
will get up again and go to my Father's house;'
may our readiness to forgive calm the fears,
deepen the trust of those who have hurt us; may
the blessing of mercy be on us.

> May the God of wonder be with us, delighting
> us with birdsong and thunder, sunrise and
> daisy, enchanting our senses, filling our hearts,
> giving us wide open eyes; for seeing the
> splendor in the humble and the majestic and
> may we open the eyes and hands and the hearts
> of the blind and the deaf and the insensitive;
> may the blessing of wonder be on us.

There is no greater blessing nor more awesome beauty
than the Eucharistic Celebration. The Eucharist is the
source and summit of our lives, the greatest mystery,
the axis of life and love. When we receive holy communion we experience a union with God, with ourselves and with others that is impossible to describe.
We are called to holiness, and to be holy is to be close
to Jesus. We should never become weary learning
about Jesus. John of the Cross advises us:

> There is much to fathom in Christ, for he is like
> an abundant mine with many recesses of treas-
> ures, so that however deep individuals go, they
> never reach the bottom, but rather in every
> recess find new veins with new richness every-
> where. On this account St Paul said of Christ:
> 'In Christ dwells all treasures and wisdom.'⁷

Christ gives us himself in the Eucharist, and we are
nourished and filled with his mercy and his love. We
take that mercy and love and instill it into society.
Teresa of Avila tells us how this is done: 'We cannot
be sure if we are loving God, but we can know quite
well if we are loving our neighbor. And be certain that,
the farther advanced you find you are in this, the
greater the love you will have for God.' Each time we
receive communion we become a little more like Jesus
by being more loving. At communion we receive the

grandest of gifts and through it we learn to be grateful for the smallest in the ordinary. Faith in Christ's Eucharistic presence is the most holy and most blessed mystery of love.

Christ with us
In the flame of your Eucharistic love
Illumine our faith in your passion,
Death and resurrection.

Christ with us
In the furnace of your Eucharistic love
Melt the coldness of our hearts
And burn away indifference from our lives.

Christ with us
In the fire of your Eucharistic love
Consume the sin that keeps us
From intimacy with you.

Christ with us
In the heart of your Eucharistic love
Bake us like finest bread
And break us for those
Who hunger for you. Amen.[8]

Notes

[1]   E. Wheeler Wilcox, 'Worthwhile'.

[2]   Pope John Paul II, *Discourse at Audience for the General Chapter of the Carmelites* (23 September 1995).

[3]   Karl Rahner, *Theological Investigations* 20, p. 149.

[4]   Poem by Catherine Janssen Irwin.

[5]   Pope John Paul II, *Letter to Women* (1995), 2.

[6]   *Ibid.*, 12.

[7]   St John of the Cross, *The Spiritual Canticle*, Stanza 37, 4. See also Colossians 2:3.

[8]   Croist Linn, Divine Master Convent, Stillorgan, Dublin.

BIBLIOGRAPHY

Batzdorff, Susanne (trans.), *An Edith Stein Daybook, To Live in the Hand of the Lord*. Springfield, IL: Templegate Publishers, 1994.

Christopher, Kenneth (ed.), *A Sampler of Devotional Poems*. Mahwah, NJ: Paulist Press, 1997.

Clark, John, O.C.D. (Trans.), *Story of a Soul, the Autobiography of St Therese of Lisieux*. Washington DC: ICS Publications, 1975.

de Meester, Conrad, O.C.D. (Ed.), *St Therese of Lisieux, Her Life, Times and Teaching*. Washington, DC: ICS Publications, 1997.

Dubay, Thomas, S.M., *Teresa of Avila, Personality and Prayer*, Eternal Word Television Network Video Series. San Francisco, CA: Ignatius Press, 1996.

Groeschel, Benedict, C.F.R., PhD., *Spiritual Passages The Psychology of Spiritual Development*. New York, NY: Crossroad Publishing Co, 1983.

Humphreys, Carolyn, O.C.D.S., 'Woman of Mystery', *Carmelite Digest*, Vol. 2, No. 3, Summer 1987.

Kavanaugh, Kieran, O.C.D. and Rodriguez, Otilio, O.C.D. (trans.), *The Collected Works of St. John of the Cross*. Washington, DC: ICS Publications, 1979.

Lawrence of the Resurrection, O.C.D., *The Practice of the Presence of God*. New York, NY: Doubleday, 1977.

McClernon, John (arr.), *Sermon in a Sentence*, Vol. 1. *St Therese of Lisieux*. San Francisco, CA: Ignatius Press, 2002.

Spitzer Robert, S.J., *Suffering and the God of Love*. Birmingham, AL: Eternal Word Television Network Home Video, 2005.

Vann, Gerald, O.P., *Heart of Compassion, The Vocation of Women Today*. Manchester, NH: Sophia Institute Press, 1998.

von Hildebrand, Alice, *The Privilege of Being a Woman*. Ypsilanti, MI: Veritas Press, 2002.

Walsh, Catherine Thomas, O.C.D., *My Beloved, The Story of a Carmelite Nun*. New York, NY: McGraw-Hill Book Company, 1954.

Welch, John, O. Carm., *The Carmelite Way: An Ancient Path for Today's Pilgrim*. Mahwah, NJ: Paulist Press, 1996.

Willard, Helen and Spackman, Clare, *Occupational Therapy* (Fourth Edition), Philadelphia & Toronto: J. B. Lippincott Co, 1971.